Teaching Europea

Georg Weisseno, Valentin Eck (Eds.)

Teaching European Citizens

A Quasi-experimental Study in Six Countries

In cooperation with
Henk Dekker (Leiden), Reinhold Gaertner (Innsbruck),
Bernhard Natter (Innsbruck), Audrey Osler (Leeds),
Volker Reinhardt (Luzern), Sanne A.M. Rijkhoff (Leiden),
Nicola Savvides (Leeds), Marti Taru (Tallinn),
Raivo Vetik (Tallinn), Béatrice Ziegler (Aarau)

Waxmann 2009
Münster / New York / München / Berlin

Bibliographic information published by die Deutsche Nationalbibliothek
Die Deutsche Nationalbibliothek lists this publication in the
Deutsche Nationalbibliografie; detailed bibliographic data
are available in the internet at http://dnb.d-nb.de.

This project has been funded with support from the European
Commission. This publication reflects the views only of the authors, and
the Commission cannot be held responsible for any use which may be
made of the information contained therein.

Education and Culture

Socrates

The participation of the Swiss team has been financed by the Swiss State
Secretariat for Education and Research SER.

ISBN 978-3-8309-2178-3

© Waxmann Verlag GmbH, 2009
Postfach 8603, 48046 Münster, Germany

Waxmann Publishing Co.
P. O. Box 1318, New York, NY 10028, U. S. A.

www.waxmann.com
info@waxmann.com

Cover Design: Christian Averbeck, Münster
Cover Picture: www.photocase.com
Print: Hubert und Co., Göttingen
Printed on age-resistant paper, acid-free as per ISO 9706

Contents

Preface

Audrey Osler, Henk Dekker, Reinhold Gaertner, Volker Reinhardt,
Raivo Vetik, Georg Weisseno & Béatrice Ziegler

Teaching European Citizens: A Quasi-experimental Study in Six Countries is writ-ten by an international research team who collaborated from 2006 to 2009 to exam-ine young people's political knowledge of the European Union. The EC-funded project *Teacher Empowerment to Educate Students to Become Active European Citizens* (TEESAEC) combined research with the development of innovative cur-riculum materials.

The team created an online WebQuest, designed for independent use by students aged 13 to 15 years, accompanied by a teacher handbook, aimed to support profes-sional development. Teachers in partner schools, from Austria, Estonia, Germany, the Netherlands, Switzerland and the UK, trialled the curriculum materials with their students. Following feedback from schools, a revised version of the materials is now available: http://www.politikwiss.ph-karlsruhe.de/teesaec/

The emphasis throughout is on active European citizenship. The materials are designed to support students in grappling with sometimes complex EU processes by providing them with the necessary conceptual tools. In other words, the aim is to strengthen students' political literacy. The outcome is a resource to support teach-ers in addressing the European dimension of citizenship, so that students become informed voters and engaged European citizens.

From this followed the ambitious research agenda which is reported here in *Teaching European Citizens.* The research aims of the international project team were: to make an analysis of students' knowledge of the European Union; to assess the impact of the web-based materials on students within selected schools in each nation-state; and, finally, to assess students' learning gain in these schools. In each school, teachers made the WebQuest available to some students; a second control group completed a parallel series of lessons, using material of the teacher's own choosing. Students completed a pre-test questionnaire before commencing their studies and answered the same questionnaire following their classes, as a post-test.

The structure of the book

In chapter one of *Teaching European Citizens* Weisseno and Eck discuss the teach-ing project and some of the challenges encountered in introducing EU-related con-cepts and processes to young people. They follow this, in chapter two, with an analysis of the research data from Germany, concluding that a young person's interest in politics and academic self-concept are more strongly linked to learning gain than the actual teaching method to which s/he is exposed. In chapter three, Reinhardt, Waldis and Ziegler also consider the importance of young people's interests and attitudes in predicting learning; in this case discussing young people's study of the EU in Switzerland, a non-EU member-state, where young people are likely to be exposed to rather different political perspectives from those prevalent in Germany. In chapter four, Rijkhoff and Dekker analyze the origins of conceptual EU-knowledge and the impact of WebQuest and other lessons on this knowledge among students in the Netherlands. In chapter five, Taru analyses pre- and post-test results from students in Estonia. The Estonian teachers noted how WebQuest increased young people's levels of interest; it did not, however, prove to be a more efficient way of learning.

In Austria, by contrast, the WebQuest materials appear to have had a greater impact on student learning than the alternative teacher-led classes. Interestingly, Gaertner and Natter explore differences and similarities they uncover between young people with migration and non-migration backgrounds. The final chapter examining country-specific results is by Osler and Savvides, who report on schools in England. The British partners extended the common work plan to interview teachers about their perceptions of students' needs as learner-citizens and students' attitudes to the EU. Their results suggest that teachers in England find it difficult to reconcile their beliefs about active community-focused learning with the topic of the EU, which seems remote to students. In the final chapter, Dekker and Rijkhoff contextualize and reflect on the research results from the six countries.

The challenge remains for teachers across Europe to educate young people for tolerance and cooperation. Young people are entitled to forms of political education which enable them to look critically at alternative viewpoints. This is essential in a context where extremist groups and political parties seek to influence the young.

TEESAEC was funded by the European Commission under the Comenius action programme (Grant reference: 128741-CP-1-2006-1-DE-COMENIUS-C21). The authors extend their warm thanks to all participating teachers and schools and to their universities: University of Innsbruck, University of Leeds, Leiden University, University of Tallinn, University of Teacher Education of the Applied Sciences North-western Switzerland (Aarau), University of Teacher Education Central Switzerland (Lucerne), and Karlsruhe University of Education (coordinating partner). The authors also wish to acknowledge the full research team: Gina Aschwanden, Farah Bazzi, Katrin Hahn-Laudenberg, Tobias Heinemann, Michalis Kakos, Yvonne Leimgruber, Pippa Meer, Jolanda van der Noll, Monika Oberle, Terje Tarve, Louise Williams, and Corinne Wyss.

Concepts on the European Union – A teaching project

Georg Weisseno & Valentin Eck

The "Teacher Empowerment to Educate Students to Become Active European Citizens" (TEESAEC) project that is being promoted by the European Union from 2006 to 2009 within the framework of the Comenius Programme has two objectives. On the one hand, materials on the European Union should be put on-line in the new form of a WebQuest together with curriculum suggestions for teacher training (http://www.politikwiss.ph-karlsruhe.de/teesaec/). On the other hand, a test on knowledge is to be effected in the test run of a series of teaching lessons before and after these lessons are carried out, which is to give information on the increase in learning of students of the age of 14 to 15 via the new teaching method. The series of teaching lessons was revised on the basis of the success in learning and the evaluation of the feedback of teachers and students, and is now available in four languages. The materials have been developed jointly by six European partners.

1. Aims and formulation of questions for the series of teaching lessons

The series of teaching lessons devised provides the students with an introduction to the development of the European Union by showing the interaction of the institutions in the example of the planned CO_2 Ordinance for exhaust emissions. This practical example of the on-going legislative procedure during the period of the project shall provide the students with a closer insight in terms of transparency, comprehension and up-to-datedness, into the competences and functions of the institutions of the European Union. The cognitive approach to deal with the discussions on the new ordinance shall improve, resp. support the attitude to the EU. Since the legislative process of the EU deviates in many aspects from the processes in the member countries, the subject of learning is at any rate new for the students. Analogies to their own political system can hardly be helpful to them, and so they have to develop conceptual ideas of a general kind on democracy and on the European Union.

The perception of the EU citizenship requires to have knowledge on the European Union. The competence in politics relating to this develops when one deals with questions posed on Europe, and teaching affords a contribution to this. Agreement on the European values which are fundamental for political action within this context does not come automatically but requires knowledge that influences one's own considerations and attitudes.

What this is dependent on is that the network of European politics is clarified, thus providing the many indecisive and uninformed students the framework to form their own opinions. Given that the European Union as a subject of discussion is treated with minor importance in the family home and with friends, or at least might be backed up with comparatively little knowledge in concrete terms, an important information function is attached to the teaching at school. There, students acquire important specialist concepts of the European Union and are then able to follow the daily news and to build up further their store of knowledge independently. Knowledge can be communicated, positive basic attitudes can be developed and strengthened, the readiness for engagement promoted, and motivation to tackle European issues raised.

The series of teaching lessons is comprised of 4 learning units, having their own logical structure. They can be dealt with in 6 teaching lessons. The first teaching unit presents the content of the planned ordinance to reduce CO_2 exhaust emissions. This is explained on the basis of climate protection against the background of climate change, and reference is made to the effect that the EU is seeking to implement the resolutions in the Kyoto Protocol through this ordinance. Since the EU Commission and the EU Commissioners have initiated the legislation process (right of initiative), the task of the unit is to explain in principle their significance. Thus not all the institutions of the EU are introduced simultaneously, only the Commission as focal point first of all.

In the second teaching unit, the controversial reactions to the draft of ordinance in the Council of Ministers are analysed. It is shown that national interests of individual member states in the specific case strongly rest on the car industry (associations) that is present in the individual countries and less on the influence of environmental protection associations. It is made clear that it is important to forge alliances because individual countries can be outvoted. Without the consent of the Council of Ministers, no ordinance can be passed. Therefore the key powers of the Council of Ministers are explained, which also convenes as Council on the Environment, and prepares the resolution at the level of the specialist ministers. Thereby a further key body in the legislative process is shown in the work involved with a planned ordinance.

The next teaching unit deals with the Climate Initiative of the EU and the contributions of associations and their inclusion in the political negotiating process to solve the problem. To implement the Kyoto Protocol, a series of measures is needed which also affect the car industry. For to prepare the ordinance, a working group, to which the individual government representatives and representatives of the associations belong, advised the Commission. The report is made available as well to the parliamentarians of the European Parliament. The procedure, to especially include the representatives of the European car industry federations and the environmental protection associations, is characteristic for government action at a European level (lobbyism). Therefore it is made clear that the various associations are taking part not only in negotiations with civil servants and the members of the Commission but also take up positions publicly for to influence within their way of thinking the further adoption of resolutions in the institutions (Commission, Council of Ministers, European Parliament).

The following fourth teaching unit is the interplay of all the participatory institutions in rising complexity. First of all the European Parliament is presented in this teaching unit. As it is responsible for transportation and the environment, it is participated in the legislative procedure. The interplay of Parliament and the Council of Ministers requires that the respective majority opinions are taken into account so that the ordinance can be passed by both bodies. That is why the Parliament gets involved from the outset in the decision-making process with a debate, though a vote has to be taken only after the ordinance is passed by the Council Of Ministers. The European parties must form coalitions in the Parliament in order to influence from their side the process of opinion-forming in the Commission and in the Council of Ministers. This happens at first relatively independently of the opinion-forming process in the Council of Ministers because the parliamentary majority does not have to support the commission and the Council of Ministers is on its part independent. One can recognise from this teaching unit that in such a way a network of relationships and different interests comes into play. The European Parliament, Commission, Council of Ministers and interest groups are shown in a negotiation process that in the end produces a jointly prepared ordinance which looks at any rate different from that presented in the first teaching unit.

As a whole, the following key concepts are introduced within the course of the teaching units: car industry, EU Budget, Climate Protection, EU Commissioner, European Union, European Commission, EU Industrial Policy, EU Environmental Policy, EU Consumer Protection, EU citizen, associations, EU Legislative Procedure, Law Initiative, National Governments, European Parliament, European Elections, Votum EP, President of the European Commission, European Democracy, peace, prosperity, EU institutions, national sovereignty, European interests, national interests, tolerance, global warming, Council of Ministers, Council on the Environment, European political parties. The students are expected to have integrated by the end of the series of teaching lessons as many as possible, resp. all the concepts into their individual semantic networks.

2. Learning with concepts

The learning process is influenced by many factors as, for instance, motivation, the self-image, the level of knowledge, the model and the success in learning. All the factors have a combined effect in the brain. The learning success in school is that what matters to the teachers and students. The role of teaching is to develop cultural skills (general world knowledge) just as well as domain-specific knowledge in school subjects. The domain-specific knowledge belongs to the competence area of subject-related knowledge, in this case to the domain of political science. According to this definition, the competence in politics is determined functionally as a sub-competence, i.e. domain-specific, and is related to a confined sector of contexts and situations (Hartig & Klieme, 2006, p. 129). The competence in politics as a capability to apply domain-specific knowledge in various contexts can be tested in different ways. Factual questions can be asked or questions on conceptual knowledge. Such domain-specific or content-based knowledge, e.g. on the European Union, arise through many perception details in the brain being erased and the important relationships between elements in terms of content being stored via abstraction: "A type of abstraction exists in leaving aside specific experiences and instead categorising generally the features and characteristics of the respective class of experience. Such a type of abstraction creates conceptual knowledge which includes categories like chairs and dogs." (Anderson, 2001, p. 153)

The cognitive competence is therefore of key importance in the school subject of politics, which can be ascertained via tests of knowledge. It also assumes a prominent position in the TEESAEC project when the success in learning with the teaching method (WebQuest) is measured by the increase in knowledge. Drawn upon as a theoretical general model for the development of competences through teaching is the model of Scientific Literacy of Bybee (1997, p. 56ff.) which defines the levels of a scientific basic education and which can apply for school education. Bybees concept of general education describes basic capabilities that are necessary scientific terms (e.g. election) and of formalism

- conceptual and procedural Civic Literacy: comprehension of key political concepts and processes, establishing relationships between facts, terms and principles (e.g. federalism with the corresponding network of concepts)

- multidimensional Civic Literacy: comprehension of the special features of political-scientific thinking, capability to arrange in economic, social and cultural associations (e.g. one's own logic of the terms of power in political science and in economics).

The concept of the 'European Union' belongs to the field of politics as the concept 'dog' belongs to the field of biology. Related to the project, this means that the concept of the European Union explains a whole series of further terms, as e.g. the

Council of Ministers or the Commission, which form together a network as well as opening up the way to explain the relevance of the meaning and the purpose of the concept. Such a network is linked up in the brain with other networks on other concepts, as e.g. parliament or government. Conceptual knowledge leaves aside specific experiences and categorises instead the features and characteristics of the respective class of experience (Anderson, 2001, p. 153ff.). This categorisation is effected via semantic networks and patterns. In semantic networks, the relationships between the terms are developed. Terms are therefore not insulated in the memory but are more or less networked in a stable manner. Patterns organise extensive knowledge via typical associations.

If the standard question hitherto has run in the teaching lesson as follows: "What have we said on the European Union?", then the future question will perhaps be: "Which ideas on the European Union have been developed?" The students shall acquire conceptual knowledge; they shall not memorise charts or attempt to learn without comprehending. It must be clear at any rate which potential in competence lies in an assignment or in a lesson, which conceptual knowledge is expected from the learner in processing materials and how the solutions, resp. results are to be classified. Knowledge is to be seen in the form of activities involved with solving tasks. This means in concrete terms that the materials and learning exercises are only then suitable if they produce statements on the pre-defined specialised concepts and terms in respect of the European Union.

Which terms are to be conceptualised in which sequence and with which material, in order to attain a pre-defined increase in knowledge? This can be a guiding question in the planning of competence-orientated teaching in conjunction with the question of how to acquire general competences (e.g. motivational orientation, social competence). The orientation of the teaching and planning for empirical findings in terms of learning psychology, as the theory of situated learning, the anchored instruction approach, the cognitive flexibility approach and the cognitive apprenticeship approach, which are hardly adopted at all in the field of civic education, is required (Müller & Duit, 2004). The result from these is that new terms and concepts can be anchored in the already existing network of knowledge. The learning situation needs to facilitate the confrontation with positive and negative examples of a term through an appropriate sequencing. The identification of other (specialised) terms as being laterally arranged, superordinate, or subordinate and the use of new terms expand the spectrum of the existing individual terms of the learner. This can be explicitly referred to in the teaching. It is only in this way that students can assess the appropriateness of their own terms and develop their conceptual knowledge.

By conceiving that structures of knowledge can be interpreted as a map, a network of political terms, it is expected that they promote the processing of information effectively when one manages to identify these structures and the classifiable statements regarding them in the materials of the teaching units. "Anchorage" for political constructions are provided in the teaching, which can be relevant for one's own political decision-making and conclusions. This reminds one of the primary school teaching where the children are given a number of "learning words" to practise and use before they write a dictation or an essay.

In order to promote competence in politics, the materials have to be adapted for performance. The tasks have to fulfil several functions in respect of the materials in WebQuest. 1.) They have the effect that the learners collate and secure the messages of the material. 2.) They achieve that the learners network and repeat. 3.) They serve exploration and discovery. 4.) They provide guidance via the content. The practice is to a large extent more reflective when students have the opportunity to make discoveries. The tasks serve to solve problems and to learn individually. Given the competence-oriented choice of material and construction of tasks, which are used for the processing and which stimulate the intellect to deal with contents, WebQuest is breaking new ground. Ultimately, the students must succeed in building up their own network of terms regarding the European Union, alongside the network of terms and materials that have been pre-given and interlinked with each other. The teachers' feedback is required in order to discover correct and incorrect conceptualisations. Correct answers have to be strengthened, incorrect ones to be corrected. It is not a matter of assessing personal opinions of the students but correct answering conduct in terms of specialist knowledge. The question has to be asked whether the method chosen for the project allows to be the mixture of independent and adapted learning that is necessary for the success of learning. For if the teaching method does not suit the individual learning behaviour, the students learn less (Souvigner & Gold, 2006, p. 154). For this reason, the competence in politics of the students was ascertained before and after the teaching via a test.

3. WebQuest as a learning method

The materials selected according to the aspects of the learning-by-concepts are supplemented by the consequent implication of a learning strategy that especially fosters the competence domain of specialised knowledge through stimulating individual constructions with the help of specialised concepts and terms. It is a self-learning project in the form of a WebQuest, which is accessible to everyone on the internet. It is to be expected that the 'new' learning method additionally motivates the students. WebQuest is according to its discoverer Bernie Dodge "an inquiry-oriented activity in which some or all of the information that learners interact with comes from resources on the Internet" (1997). A key element of WebQuests is the independent processing of information on the internet via domain-specific questions, which strongly guide more or less the specific work and search orders.

It is due to WebQuest (Manzel, 2007) that solely internet sources are used as materials. Since WebQuest is equally an E-learning programme with the help of internet sources, it has to be predesigned from the aspects of learning psychology. The competence-oriented setting of tasks necessitates a clear structuring of the materials, accompanied by the terms to be acquired. The students are provided with key words (terms) which occur in the texts and which are to be integrated into their own network of knowledge. These and other terms are new and can be combined with existing ones. These are elements of a network being designed.

It is to be observed here that the learning tasks pursue solely the aim of promoting a systematic build-up of knowledge. This is to be ensured through the obligatorily prescribed materials of WebQuest coordinated to productivity, whereas the large number of voluntarily searchable links to accessory materials (photos, YouTube videos, self-presentations of players etc.) cannot completely meet the demands, because they are not chosen and arranged according to aspects of subject-related didactics. They are therefore only limitedly coordinated to prior knowledge and capabilities. They have the function of supporting one's own search behaviour for solutions. Avid users have numerous new learning opportunities via the internet sources, which consolidate and repeat the learning matter. In spite, it may be difficult for the students to differentiate between the specialist correct information and opinion-making or false assertions.

The problem of the internet-aided learning offer of WebQuest lies in the fact that it is to a high degree a learning offer geared to the individual. Though the contents in pre-structured form are offered in relatively small steps, the medial form of information provision has to be in harmony with the learning preferences in order to obtain the success in learning (Souvigner & Gold, 2006, p. 154). A large number of learning opportunities are without doubt provided, but a feedback from the teachers is absolutely necessary for to ensure the success in learning. Only then larger networks of knowledge can emerge via the self-learning processes. It has to be heeded here that the success in learning will only set in during feedback phases that are reasonable for the individual. It depends on the personal fitting of the independent and adjusted style of learning. Only the interplay of guided practice, allowing observation, rendering support and self-activity when processing the WebQuest can result in success. The more the teachers adopt the aims and contents of WebQuest as their very own and implement it appropriately for the situation, the greater shall be the effectiveness of this learning method. That is why the teachers in the partner countries were familiarised beforehand intensively with the teaching method and the teaching with concepts, in order to create the optimum conditions for to accompany the learners. The results of the empirical accompanying research shall provide indications on the effectiveness.

4. The solutions of students in WebQuest

The tasks in WebQuest ask predominantly about the contexts in the materials. This requires from the students a capacity to comprehend and retain. But they extend beyond this and demand an evaluation and assessment of the facts via inductive and deductive conclusions. A large number of facts on the institutions of the EU constitutes situations of application in WebQuest just as equal as the case of (the CO_2 Ordinance) itself, which is presented as a fundamental problem. The learning of concepts and the network of terms accompanying them together with their relations provide the facts with a clear structure and make the learning process being demanded transparent. With the help of the instructions (tasks) the learner knows what is demanded and has firstly the chance to recognise his or her misconceptions (from a specialist viewpoint these are false concepts) in the solutions. Indispensable for the learning process is, nevertheless, the personal feedback of the teacher, without which misconceptions are reinforced and proper concepts are not strengthened.

Should a student lack the exact knowledge to solve the task, he or she shall search for solution possibilities via declarative or inductive conclusions in all his/her networks. Thus a solution for a task can emerge, partly or even completely, via the concepts of head of government, state president, minister, or mayor etc., without the exact definition of the concept of EU Commissioner being available (mental model). The more situations of application the concept of EU Commissioner requires, the more extensive shall be the new network of knowledge being developed with the concept of EU Commissioner and the more extensive the domain-specific knowledge shall be through comparison with similar concepts. The more often a fact is encountered over a concept, the stronger it is associated with the concept (Anderson, 2001). When students possess conceptual knowledge over politics, they can find the right solutions for questions in situations of application as citizens, although they have had no prior experience with the correct answer required.

The lists of concepts of the specialist concept of the European Union that are published on the internet pages of WebQuest and in the teacher manual shall provide an overview on what emerged in the individual lessons and in the respective tasks. These concepts have to be used by the students correctly in the solutions. They are to be described together with further concepts in the solutions of the tasks. The specialist concept of the European Union is in no way fully reflected via this list within the sense of a political-scientific construct, but is essentially reduced for the teaching at school of Secondary Level I and at the same time restricted. So there are missing e.g. the domains of European Foreign Policy, Regional Policy, Agricultural Policy, for to name just a few.

5. Summary and Outlook

The learning by concepts and with concepts takes up a prominent position in the teaching about the European Union. Thereby the competence in politics of the students is to be strengthened. The WebQuest learning method seems to be suitable in the form presented here to produce these cognitive performances, enhance motivation and to foster independence. The accompanying research in the partner countries referred to in the following chapters will show whether the teaching methods actually bring about a higher increase in learning than an otherwise arranged teaching lesson. In the accompanying research, also some predicators of school performance were therefore controlled, as e.g. migration background, subjective knowledge on politics and attitudes to the EU. The influence of how classes were guided and of teacher behaviour were not researched.

References

Anderson, J. R. (2001). *Kognitive Psychologie* (3. edition). Heidelberg/Berlin: Spektrum Akademischer Verlag.

Bybee, R. (1997). Toward an understanding of scientific literacy. In W. Gräber & C. Bolte (Eds.), *Scientific Literacy* (p. 37−68). Kiel: IPN.

Hartig, J. & Klieme, E. (2006). Kompetenz und Kompetenzdiagnostik. In K. Schweizer (Ed.), *Leistung und Leistungsdiagnostik* (p. 127–143). Heidelberg: Springer.

Manzel, S. (2007). *Kompetenzzuwachs im Politikunterricht. Ergebnisse einer Interventionsstudie zum Kernkonzept Europa.* Muenster: Waxmann.

Mueller, C. T. & Duit, R. (2004). Die unterrichtliche Sachstruktur als Indikator für Lernerfolg. Analyse von Sachstrukturdiagrammen und ihr Bezug zu Leistungsergebnissen im Physikunterricht. *Zeitschrift für Didaktik der Naturwissenschaften,* 10, 147–161.

Seel, N. M. (2003). *Psychologie des Lernens.* Lehrbuch für Pädagogen und Psychologen (2. ed.). München/Basel: Ernst Reinhardt.

Souvigner, E. & Gold, A. (2006). Förderung von Leistung. In K. Schweizer (Ed.), *Leistung und Leistungsdiagnostik* (p. 145–186). Heidelberg: Springer.

Weisseno, G. (2007). Kompetenzmodell. In G. Weisseno, K.-P. Hufer, H.-W. Kuhn, P. Massing & D. Richter (Eds.), *Wörterbuch politische Bildung* (p. 175–182). Schwalbach: Wochenschau.

Political knowledge of 14- to 15-year-old students – Results of the TEESAEC intervention study in Germany

Valentin Eck & Georg Weisseno

1. Theoretical framework and state of research

Of particular importance for the development of knowledge in a specific content area (domain) the acquisition of terms (concepts) as well as insight into the networks between them (conceptual knowledge) (e.g., Byrnes & Wasik, 1991, p. 777; Rittle-Johnson & Siegler, 1998, p. 77; Rittle-Johnson, Siegler & Alibali, 2001). Theories on conceptual change (see Vosniadou & Brewer, 1992) are grounded in the assumption that learning processes are influenced by the pre-existing concepts of the learner. Inadequate or false concepts are described as misconceptions, prior beliefs, or alternative frameworks. During the learning process, knowledge is actively constructed and networked on the basis of these pre-existing concepts (Duit, 1995).

Empirical political-science studies on knowledge elaborate in particular upon factual knowledge focusing on the association between knowledge and attitudes (Delli Carpini & Keeter, 1996; Galston, 2001). There is evidence to suggest that knowledge level has particularly positive effects on attitudes towards migrants as well as on readiness to participate (Popkin & Dimock, 1999). Moreover, an association has been found between the duration of politics education in school and the development of pro-democratic attitudes (Nie, Junn & Stehlik-Barry, 1996). In contrast, studies conducted by Biedermann (2006) and the International Association for the Evaluation of Educational Achievement (IEA) Study (Torney-Purta et al., 2001) both demonstrated that state of knowledge hardly correlates with political attitudes and convictions.

Regarding teaching methods and knoweldge aquisition, an intervention study has demonstrated increased effectiveness of learning with the internet-based self-instructional teaching method of WebQuest (Manzel, 2007).

The current study persues this question, too, with a different methical design. Does the use of WebQuest as a self-instructional tool lead to a greater increase in knowledge as compared with a purely teacher-controlled teaching environment?

2. Factors influencing students' political knowledge

In the current study, predictors of knowledge on the European Union are theoretically derived from results of previous empirical studies. Prior knowledge represents the starting point for the current intervention and must later be taken into account when assessing increases in knowledge. The aim of the study is to determine which student characteristics help to predict the degree of conceptual knowledge possessed by the students before the series of teaching lessons was conducted (see the article of Weisseno & Eck, Concepts on the European Union in the present volume). The study accordingly focuses on the effects of these characteristics on students' (1) prior knowledge and (2) increase in knowledge. In the following sections, the variables which are assumed to influence political knowledge and which were employed in the present study are presented and the expected effects of these variables are outlined (see Table 1).

Numerous political-science studies have generally found that women have a more distant relationship to politics than men. Women participate less in politics and display a lower degree of both political interest and knowledge. Institutional and socio-economic factors as well as factors of political culture and socialisation are assumed to be responsible for this difference between the sexes (Westle & Schoen, 2002).

Since students from both year 9 of *Realschulen* (lower-track secondary high schools) and year 10 of *Gymnasien* (higher-track secondary high schools) participated in the present study, differences in performance were controlled for by including this variable in analyses. Age can be expected to influence political knowledge in connection with differing levels of cognitive development and varying durations of education (Walter, Senkbeil, Rost, Carstensen & Prenzel, 2006).

School-performance studies (PISA, IGLU, IEA) have also found that students with a migration background have lower competences in mathematics, the natural sciences, and reading (Baumert, Stanat & Watermann, 2006). Migration background can thus be expected to have a negative influence on prior knowledge and the acquisition of knowledge.

The number of books at home serves as a proxy measure of the cultural capital of students' parents and has proven useful in numerous school-performance studies. In the tradition of Tocqueville, associations/clubs can be seen to represent "schools of democracy"; social capital theory postulates that social networks foster trust and democratic standards and values among their members from which advantages arise for the individual and for the co-habitation of people (Putnam, 1994, 2001; Gabriel, Roßteutscher, Kunz & van Deth, 2002).

Interest in politics as a dispositional characteristic is a key prerequisite for learning success in this specialist domain. Intrinsic interest leads to a self-determined approach to the subject and promotes self-instructional learning beyond the class-room (Schiefele, 1996).

Academic self-concepts as personal psychological features are also known to foster performance at school (Köller & Baumert, 2001). This effect is conveyed through the student's performance: only students who are principally convinced that they are able to solve a task sum up the necessary endurance and cognitive re-sources for successful task completion, whereas individuals with a low self-concept tend to avoid task engagement (Helmke & Weinert, 1997).

According to the findings of research on educational approaches to democracy, democratic behaviour in schools increases competence in politics and respective knowledge components (McDevitt & Kiousis, 2006).

The concept of latent learning assumes that knowledge is automatically and un-intentionally obtained through the consumption of certain media. Students who ex-clusively examine the sports section of a newspaper or solely watch entertainment programmes on television can nevertheless passively or unconsciously obtain po-litically relevant information. It can therefore be presumed that media use results in greater prior knowledge. In the face of the empirical findings presented above the following effects are expected in the current study.

Table 1
Summary of predictors and expected effects on the criterion variables

Predictor	Theoretical background	Expected effect on prior knowledge	Expected effect on increase in knowledge
WebQuest	Manzel, 2007		+
Sex	Westle, 2002	−	
School year	Walter, Senkbeil, Rost, Carstensen & Prenzel, 2006	+	
Migration background	Baumert, Stanat, & Watermann, 2006	−	−
Number of books	Bourdieu, 1979	+	+
Membership in associations/clubs	Putnam 1994, 2001; Coleman, 1988	+	+
Interest in politics	Rössl & Beckert-Zieglschmid, 2002	+	+
Self-concept	Köller, Schabel & Baumert, 2000	+	+
Democratic class climate	McDevitt & Kiousis, 2006	+	+

3. Design of the intervention study

The TEESAEC project contains an intervention study in which teaching with WebQuest was compared with a teacher-controlled teaching unit in year 9 of the *Realschule* and year 10 of the *Gymnasium* (22 classes). With respect to the study sample, the data set used here solely included students who had taken part in both the pre-test and the post-test in order to allow for the measurement of individual changes. The first measurement occasion included data on a total of 572 students, 502 of whom also provided data on the second measurement occasion. This corresponds to an attrition rate of approximately 12%, which can be seen as rather low. This attrition results from the fact that some students were not present for the post-test or the pre-test or from difficulties assigning the observations to a certain person. The sample comprised 292 boys (58%) and 210 girls.

Data regarding knowledge on the European Union was acquired using a standardised questionnaire which was completed in written form. The questionnaire contained a knowledge test with questions in a traditional multiple-choice format. Students were required to select one of four answer options in response to each question. In order to check the comprehensibility and solvability of the questions, a pilot test was conducted. Besides the knowledge test, the questionnaire also contained questions on socio-demographic background variables as well as on further characteristics of the respondents. Questionnaires were to be completed within 45 minutes on both measurement occasions.

4. Construction of the measurement model

When measuring knowledge, appropriate scaling is required because it is not the specific response behaviour to single questions which is of interest. Instead, personal ability is to be determined on the basis of responses to all questions and in a way which allows inter-individual comparisons. The ability of an individual cannot be directly observed and is therefore regarded as a latent variable. In line with traditional test theory, a latent personal characteristic comprises the total score of a test plus measurement error. No distinction is made here between latent and manifest (observable) variables. The characteristic of the person is is therefore equal to the response behaviour; special emphasis is attached to estimation of the measurement error.

According to item response theory, latent personal ability is estimated on the basis of probabilistic assumptions. Decisive for correct responses to a question is the ability of the person (person parameter) on the one hand and the difficulty of the question (item parameter) on the other. The probability that a person with a certain ability level provides the correct answer is estimated for each question. The probability of solving a question is therefore a function of the person parameter and the item parameter. In our case, dichotomous answer variables were employed (correct vs. incorrect answer).

In selecting the measurement models, we drew upon three assumptions: (1) All knowledge questions measure the same characteristic and load onto the general factor "knowledge on the EU". From the outset, questions which were correctly answered by more than 95% or less than 25% of the students were omitted. The first assumption of one-dimensionality was examined with the help of two-parametrical IRT models for each of the two measurement occasions and items were excluded which did not significantly load onto the general factor. The selected model showed good data fit for the pre-test and the post-test.

(2) The measurement model is independent of group membership. To test this second assumption, sex and migration background were investigated (group-specific measurement invariance) using a multi-group model. Parameters were estimated separately for boys and girls as well as for persons with and without a migration background. We excluded items for which group-specific factor loadings differed from the overall model by more than .30. We were thus able to constrain item parameters to be equal across groups. Accordingly, the probability of solving a specific question is equally high for boys and for girls with the same ability and does not depend on migration background.

(3) The scale for knowledge measurement can be used in both the pre-test and the post-test. Item parameters are therefore identical in both tests (time-specific measurement variance). In order to ensure that knowledge on both measurement occasions can be measured using a standardised scale, item parameters were equally set, with knowledge on both occasions being conceived of as two-dimensional. Item parameters from this joint scaling were compared with separately scaled parameters, and items with standardised item parameters which deviated from the joint scaling by more than 0.30 were excluded. The measurement model with equally set parameters accordingly did not significantly differ from a non-restrictive model and shows good data fit. The latent correlation between the two tests was strikingly high, amounting to $r = .87$. Figure 1 illustrates the final measurement model with 34 indicators (Figure 1).

As an indication of the external validity of the measurements, students provided their last school grade in the subject of social studies. In addition, respondents were asked to estimate how much they knew about the European Union using a 10-point scale. The correlation between last school grade and knowledge was $\rho = -.206$ at pre-test and $\rho = -.225$ at post-test (Spearman's Rho, resp. $p<.001$; the negative coefficient is due to the reciprocal scaling of the school grades.) This association is not especially high. As mentioned above, however, the applied test clearly represents a different type of knowledge test than class work, so that a high association was not expected.

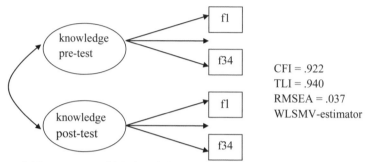

Figure 1. Measurement model for knowledge at pre-test and post-test with item parameters constrained to be equal across both occasions, as indicated by identical numeration. The variance of the latent variable was fixed to 0.

5. Results of the regression analysis for prior knowledge

The following results were obtained using multivariate latent regression analyses with maximum-likelihood estimation and prior knowledge as dependent variable. Adding the independent variables in a step-by-step manner allows insight into the causal structure between the factors of influence.

Model 1 contains sex, migration background, school year, and experimental group. Here, students in WebQuest classes show significantly higher pre-knowledge on the EU than students in controlled classes. This effect becomes insignificant in model 2 (see Table 2). As expected, classes from the higher-track *Gymnasium* also show more prior knowledge than those from the lower-track *Realschule*. No significant difference is found between girls and boys.

Migration background, as measured by language spoken at home and parents' country of origin has a weak influence which disappears in model 2. When country of origin is controlled for, no significant effect of language is seen. Effects of migration background on pre-knowledge on the EU thus can not exclusively be explained by a lack of language competence; other integration aspects associated with the country of origin are also likely to play a role. When comparing countries of origin, students with at least one parent who was born in Turkey or Eastern Europe fare a little worse than fellow students with German parents. For Eastern Europe, however, this effect is no longer significant in model 2 and 3. Disadvantages related to migration background seem to take effect rather indirectly via cultural capital and political interest.

Table 2

DV: Pre-test knowledge	Model 1	Model 2	Model 3
School year: 10	**.385***	**.366***	**.352***
Experimental group: WebQuest	**.156***	.112	.098
Sex: female	-.107	-.016	-.023
Parents' country of origin (Reference category: Germany)			
Turkey	**-.129***	**-.090***	**-.099***
Southern Europe	-.065	.003	-.062
Eastern Europe	**-.147***	-.081	-.007
other	-.059	-.043	.010
Languages spoken at home (Reference category: only German)			
German and other	.071	.014	.008
only other	.031	.020	.006
Number of books at home		**.133***	**.095***
Membership in			
youth organisations		.062	**.115****
political & social organisations		.020	.028
sport clubs & cultural organisations		.024	.013
Interest in politics			
regarding Germany		**.400***	.069
regarding the EU		.000	.059
Self-concept for talent			**.297***
Democratic classroom climate			-.048
Use of media			
TV			-.061
daily newspaper			**.114***
magazines			-.034
radio			-.012
Internet			**.107****
R^2	**.237**	**.401**	**.436**

In model 2, interest in politics, the number of books at home, and membership in associations/clubs are included (Table 2). The more books the parents have in their household, the higher students' prior knowledge on the EU. This effect becomes insignificant in model 3. With respect to interest in politics, a positive influence is found for interest in German politics, while interest, in particular in European politics, does not explain any additional variance. Membership in different types of associations/clubs has no statistically significant impact.

The most important factor of influence is self-concept for specialised talent (model 3). If pre-test knowledge is held constant, students with more positive self-concepts regarding talent in social studies are found to achieve higher knowledge scores at post-test. Motivation and self-confidence play a key role in this explanation model. When self-concept is controlled for, the effect of interest in politics persists. The consumption of other media has a tendentially negative but non-significant effect.

A democratic teaching climate does not significantly contribute to an explanation of the variance in pre-knowledge when other variables are controlled for.

The proportion of explained variance almost doubles from model 1 (22.7%) to model 3 (43%) and is, on the whole, rather high. Nevertheless, a downward correction must be considered owing to the large number of independent variables.

6. Results of the regression analysis for knowledge increase

In order to examine the influence of the examined predictors on knowledge increase, an autoregressive model was used in which pre-test knowledge was also employed as an independent variable in the model. Regression coefficients can accordingly be interpreted as effects on knowledge change. The results are residuals which express how high increases in knowledge would be if students had all produced the same pre-test results (Prenzel, Carstensen, Schöps & Maurischat, 2006, p. 43f.).

In particular when the increase between pre- and post-test knowledge is low, pre-test performance as a control variable explains an enormous share of post-test knowledge, as a result of which interpretation of R^2 in such an autoregressive model becomes difficult (Table 3). Overall, the regression models contain very few significant effects. Girls attain better results than boys in the post-test when their prior knowledge is controlled for. However, this difference disappears in model 3. Students from the higher-track *Gymnasien* (year 10) show greater increases than those from lower-track *Realschulen* (year 9).

Table 3

DV: post-test knowledge	Model 1	Model 2	Model 3
Pre-test knowledge	.630***	.605***	.631***
School year: 10	.188**	.193**	.126*
Experimental group: WebQuest	.018	.035	-.044
Sex: female	.127*	.130*	.078
Parents' country of origin (Reference category: Germany)			
Turkey	-.043	-.029	-.039
Southern Europe	.032	.049	-.042
Eastern Europe	-.122*	-.114	-.019
other	-.045	-.044	-.024
Languages spoken at home: (Reference category: only German)			
German and other	-.041	-.036	-.007
only other	.039	-.037	.045
Number of books at home		.048	.095*
Membership in			
youth organisations		-.049	.014
political & social organisations		.057	.011
sport clubs & cultural organisations		.157*	.084*
Interest in politics			
regarding Germany		.088	-.005
regarding the EU		.036	-.052
Self-concept for talent			.156**
Democratic class climate			-.048
Use of media			
TV			-.012
daily newspaper			-.025
magazines			.002
radio			-.011
Internet			-.005
R^2	.472	.480	.555

The WebQuest variable has no significant effect. Therefore, the working hypothesis cannot be confirmed. No significant difference is found in knowledge increase between the experimental groups. The WebQuest method is thus not superior to the teacher-based methods with respect to the individual's increase in knowledge and the results therefore provide no evidence to suggest added value of self-learning stressed in education programmes.

Students who are members of sport clubs or cultural organisations seem to benefit more from the series of teaching lessons. This finding is in unison with the theory of social capital, which states that relevant information is better disseminated through integration in social networks.

The strongest influence on knowledge increase is also exerted by self-concept for specialised talent. When holding pre-test performance constant, individuals with greater confidence in their individual talent in the area of social studies attain higher scores at post-test. This supports the considerable influence which affective motivational factors have on school performance.

Use of media, political interest, and democratic climate do not independently contribute to the variance in knowledge increase.

7. Summary and discussion

Empirical evidence for superiority of the self-learning concept remains rather low and was not supported by the data of the present study. This may be due to a suboptimal mixture of self-learning and adapted learning (p. 15ff. in this volume). Alternatively, it may be due to the fact that teachers' feedback behaviour was not controlled for and that that instructions required by students were not adequately provided. From a scientific point of view, the validity of these hypotheses must be subjected to more intensive investigation.

A uniform influence of sex was not found in the present study. While girls clearly benefited more from the series of teaching lessons, sex had no large effect on pre-knowledge. The findings thus support the general discussion on the importance of sex variables in research on learning while not allowing for clear conclusions. Non-uniform results with respect to the effect of sex are likely to be found according to school subject and research design.

Results regarding the influence of migration background are in line with general findings from educational research and statistics on social affairs. Youths with a migration background perform only slightly weaker than those without such a background. In our study, migration background was ascertained based on the languages spoken at home and the parents' country of origin and was found to have a rather small overall influence. Controlling for country of origin led to a non-significant effect of the language spoken at home. These findings are problematic if one assumes that knowledge on politics and the EU is a precondition for successful participation in the political life of the community at large. The task of teaching politics and stimulating an expansion of knowledge in this domain appears to be insufficiently fulfilled here.

Self-concept for specialist talent plays a key role in the acquisition of political knowledge. The results of the study suggest that motivation and subjective specialised talent constitute factors which have a greater influence on teaching efficiency than selection of the teaching method itself. It would appear that this finding is not sufficiently taken into account in everyday teaching practices.

While social features of origin may be stable and can hardly be externally modified, there are other areas which are changeable and which may potentially influence students' acquisition of political knowledge. The results of the study indicate that the following issues warrant particular attention when it comes to didactics and teaching in social studies: the promotion of students with a migration background. In this context, the general concepts of intercultural education which have so far been employed appear to have had little effect on teaching. The development of a subject-related concept of intercultultural education is still to come. Students with a weaker self-concept for the specialised talent have hitherto not been focused upon in the didactics of social studies and have not been adequately strengthened in the teaching of politics. Concepts for the promotion of subjective specialist talent in politics must be developed. Even if such a self-concept effect is subject to socialisation, teaching can surely make a difference.

Furthermore, follow-up studies should examine whether teachers' behaviour is sufficiently geared toward fostering learning. So far, there has been no valid study on teachers of politics. Such a reasearch project may also help to further elucidate the predictors of learning, which have been investigated in the present study. A further goal should be the development of more subject-specific activities which promote learning.

References:

Baumert, J., Stanat, P. & Watermann, R. (2006) (Eds.). *Herkunftsbedingte Disparitäten im Bildungswesen.* Wiesbaden: VS-Verlag.

Byrnes, J.P. & Wasik, B.A. (1991). Role of conceptual knowledge in mathematical procedural learning. *Developmental Psychology,* 27, 777−787.

Delli Carpini, M.X. & Keeter, S. (1996). *What Americans know about politics and why it matter.* New Haven: Yale Univ. Press.

Duit, R. (1995). Empirische physikdidaktische Unterrichtsforschung. *Unterrichtswissenschaft,* 23, 98−106.

Gabriel, O.W., Kunz, V., Roßteutscher, S. & van Deth, J.W. (2002). *Sozialkapital und Demokratie. Zivilgesellschaftliche Ressourcen im Vergleich.* Wien: WUV Univ.-Verl.

Galston, W.A. (2001). Political knowledge, political engagement, and civic education. *Annual Review of Political Science,* 4, 217–234.

Helmke, A. & Weinert, F.E. (1997). Bedingungsfaktoren schulischer Leistungen. In F.E. Weinert (Ed.), *Psychologie des Unterrichts und der Schule. Enzyklopädie der Psychologie.* Themenbereich D, Serie I, Bd. 3. Goettingen: Hogrefe.

Köller, O. & Baumert, J. (2001). Leistungsgruppierungen in der Sekundarstufe I. Ihre Konsequenzen für die Mathematikleistung und das mathematische Selbstkonzept der Begabung. *Zeitschrift für Pädagogische Psychologie,* 15, 99–110.

Kulik, J.A., Kulik, C.L. & Bangert-Drowns, R.L. (1985). The importance of outcome studies: A reply to Clark. *Journal of Educational Computing Research,* 1, 381–387.

Manzel, S. (2007). *Kompetenzzuwachs im Politikunterricht: Ergebnisse einer Interventionsstudie zum Kernkonzept Europa.* Muenster/New York: Waxmann.

McDevitt, M. & Kiousis, S. (2006). Deliberative learning. An evaluative approach to interactive civic education. *Communication Education, 55 (3),* 247–264.

Prenzel, M., Carstensen, C.H., Schöps, K. & Maurischat, C. (2006). Die Anlage des Längsschnitts bei PISA 2003. In PISA-Konsortium Deutschland (Ed.), *PISA 2003: Untersuchungen zur Kompetenzentwicklung im Verlauf eines Schuljahres* (pp. 29–62). Muenster: Waxmann.

Putnam, R.D. (2000). *Bowling Alone. The collapse and revival of American community.* New York: Simon & Schuster.

Putnam, R.D. (1994). *Making democracy work. Civic traditions in modern Italy.* Princeton NJ: Princeton Univ. Press.

Rittle-Johnson, B., Siegler, R.S. & Alibali, M.W. (2001). Developing conceptual understanding and procedural skill in mathematics. An iterative process. *Journal of Educational Psychology,* 93, 346-362.

Rössel, J. & Beckert-Zieglschmid, C. (2002). Die Reproduktion kulturellen Kapitals. *Zeitschrift für Soziologie, 31,* 497–513.

Schiefele, U. (1996). *Motivation und Lernen mit Texten.* Goettingen: Hogrefe.

Vosniadou, S. & Brewer, W.F. (*1992*). Mental models of the earth: A study of conceptual change in childhood. *Cognitive Psychology,* 24, 535–585.

Walter, O., Senkbeil, M., Rost, J., Carstensen, C.H. & Prenzel, M. (2006). Die Entwicklung der naturwissenschaftlichen Kompetenz von der neunten zur zehnten Klassenstufe: Deskriptive Befunde. In PISA-Konsortium Deutschland (Ed.), *Pisa 2003. Untersuchungen zur Kompetenzentwicklung im Verlauf eines Schuljahres* (p. 87–118). Muenster: Waxmann.

Westle, B. & Schoen, H. (2001). Ein neues Argument in einer alten Diskussion. Politikverdrossenheit als Ursache des gender-gap im politischen Interesse. In F. Brettschneider, J. van Deth & E. Roller (Ed.), *Ende der politisierten Sozialstruktur?* (p. 215–244). Opladen: Leske & Budrich.

Knowledge, interest and attitudes – Results from the TEESAEC intervention study in Switzerland

Volker Reinhardt, Monika Waldis & Béatrice Ziegler

1. Theoretical framework

In this presentation, the knowledge, interest and attitudes of young people in Switzerland in respect of the European Union are reported upon. Data were collected and processed in analogy to the international data of the TEESAEC study. The results of the research are all the more significant as they elucidate the situation in a non-EU country. Beside of this, questions are asked on the effectiveness of the chosen intervention. It is examined whether an expansion in the knowledge has occurred and whether changes have emerged in the attidudes towards the EU.

The Swiss sub-study follows the design of the Karlsruhe study. Thus it assumes the theoretical conceptualization of the development of knowledge as an acquisition of concepts and their integration into a conceptual framework. As factors of influence variables such as sex, nationality, migration status and socio-cultural background of the family as well as the general interest in political contents (policy) come into question.

In Switzerland, the state of research is neither ample on knowledge about politics nor on positions on politics, knowledge and attitudes vis-à-vis (the EU)-Europe. So far, only few empirical studies have been devoted to this topic. A first overview was provided by Biedermann (2007, p. 28ff.), who had found out about and summarized five larger and smaller studies for Switzerland. He states that quantitative research into Civic Education has been accorded a rather low significance until now (p. 29).

The IEA study "Civic Education" is the research project that has been given the most attention in the area of Civic Education in recent years (see Torney-Purta et al. 2001). Based on pre-studies in some participating countries about the situation of Civic Education, the three topics 'democracy: principles, institutions and practices', 'national identity, regional and international relations' and 'social cohesion and heterogeneity' represent the principles which were ascertained in respect of the fields of knowledge, comprehension, conceptual understanding, attitudes as well as present and future-expected political practices (Biedermann, 2007, p. 29f.).

The study has brought to the surface that in Switzerland, in spite of democratic traditions and practices, the preparation of the next generation for the role of citizens cannot be considered in any way optimal. Summing up, this study shows

- that in international comparison (28 countries), 14- to 15-year-old students in Switzerland possess an average knowledge of politics, that they classify the concept of citizenship and the thereof associated duties of citizens as of little significance, express only a modest political interest, show little social engagement and voice hardly any readiness to get involved in politics in the future (Oser & Biedermann, 2003);
- that in international comparison (14 countries), 17- to 18-year-old young people from the German-speaking part of Switzerland express little interest in politics, show little readiness for future political engagement and manifest (rather) negative attitudes towards migrants as well as to their own nation, that the latter, however, – also in comparison with the 14- to 15-year-old German-speaking Swiss youths – possess a pronounced knowledge of politics, classify the roles and duties of citizens as important, engage themselves on average for the interests of society and have an extremely high trust in state and political bodies (Amadeo et al., 2002; Biedermann, 2005).

In a national supplementary project of the IEA study Civic Education, it could be shown that with the 17- to 18-year-olds in the German-speaking part of Switzerland there are various interrelations between experiences from participation in the everyday life and self- or social competences. However, no relations between participative experience and aspects of political identity (concepts, attitudes, knowledge, interest, engagement) could be ascertained (see Biedermann, 2006).

As a result of a study financed by the National Funds on the "development of political cognitions" (Oser et al., 2005), it can be upheld that knowledge, age, education and socio-economic status have a fundamental influence on the demos- and ethnos-orientation and that the largest development thrusts take place in respect of political cognition at the age of 16 and 17. An expansion of knowledge and a higher level of education is here associated with an increase in the demos-orientation and a decrease in the ethnos-centring (arrogance, national pride) (Oser et al., 2005, p. 129).

The 11th CH-X study that was carried out within the framework of the Swiss interviewing of young people and recruits put the focus of attention on Civic Education, whereby the average 20-year-old recruits and other persons of the same age cohort (especially women) were questioned and tested on their political orientation, activities and knowledge, interest in politics, political maturity as well as the teaching of politics at school. The results show that the interest in politics confined to the area of the state is low, there is a deficiency in knowledge, little readiness for engagement is expressed, and the trust in political institutions is high (Klöti & Risi, 1991, quote from Biedermann, 2007, p. 33). These results were confirmed not only by the above-cited IEA study "Civic Education", but also by the recent CH-X study, in which once again knowledge of and interest in politics were analysed. In this study 94% of the respondents supported equal opportunities for men and women. Those questioned were in favour of granting approximatively the same rights that the Swiss had to migrants (male and female) in the area of work, in the choice of partners, and in the lifestyle, but were more sceptical when it was a matter of the right of co-determination in politics. Interest in and knowledge of politics among young people turned out to be relatively low on average. Only 5% were very strongly interested in political affairs, 24% not at all. Of the total nine questions of knowledge on politics, the average of the respondents could only answer 4 correctly (see Bieri, Buschor & Forrer, 2005).

A small sub-study of a Swiss long-term study on "early reading and early calculation" started in 1995, evaluated in 2003 the answers of 16-year-olds to questions on their interest in and attitudes towards Europe (Stamm, 2007, p. 385ff.). Questions were asked in four sub-scales on the "identification with Europe", "comprehension of Europe", "openness towards Europe" and "Europe as a chance for one's own personal future" with the help of three items each. In addition, attitudes were investigated to the participation at school with the help of scales on the "confidence in the effectiveness of participation at school" and the "free expression of opinion in the classroom". It can be stated as the result on the "identification with Europe" that young people in all school levels identify clearly stronger with Switzerland than with Europe, and therefore discuss from a marked national perspective (p. 388). Furthermore, only every fifth or sixth respondent was familiar to some extent with the political functions of the EU or rather was interested in them. Most of the young people had solely an utilitarian interest in Europe, being aware of it particularly through the then newly introduced euro. The "openness towards Europe" was reflected in a large interest in other cultures. Moreover, a division was evident in regard to the willingness to accept migrants and refugees seeking political asylum: every third grammar school student was strongly in favour of accepting them, but only one-sixth of the students from other secondary and secondary modern schools were so (p. 390f.). Regarding having a personal future in association with Europe, there were a rightly large group of grammar school students who were prepared to move inside Europe and a clearly less mobility-geared group of other secondary and secondary modern schools' students. Questioned on the possibilities for participation at school, 55 percent of the students from secondary and secondary modern schools and 67 percent of the students from grammar schools said that they had the possibility to express their opinions freely, but only about half of the students in the grammar school and about a third in the secondary and secondary modern school were able to perceive that they could participate effectively in a marked manner at school. Summing up, Margrit Stamm stated for the sub-study that young people associated their interest in Europe particularly with personal usage and grammar school students were far more open-minded towards Europe in all spheres than young people from "types of school with lower requirements". The positive attitudes towards the possibilities to participate at school had, on the whole, positive effects on an "open Europe" (p. 395).

2. Institutional framework: Teaching at secondary 1-level in Switzerland

Students are taught in Switzerland in accordance with the cantonal education system, curricula and prescribed or officially approved teaching materials. At present, there are efforts underway to adapt the cantonal education system in terms of structure and content to the compulsory years of school. Regarding our survey, however, the educational organizations of the cantons of Aargau and Lucerne are applicable where the questioning was undertaken.

In the canton of Aargau, the transfer into the secondary modern, secondary or district school[1] (ascending in respect of performance requirements) takes place after the fifth school year. The compulsory years of school end with the full completion of the ninth school year. In the canton of Lucerne, various school models ensue after six years of primary school. They extend from a comprehensive school to a school model with four different levels split up from A (highest level) to D (lowest level). Besides, there is the possibility to transfer to a long-term grammar school.[2]

'The syllabus in Aargau does not explicitly provide for Civic Education. In the secondary and district schools a transdisciplinary unit called "*Soziale Mitwelt*" that binds together Geography, History and Ethics/Religion(s) requires the fostering of self- and social competency. In respect of the secondary modern school, orientation in the world of work and career perspectives is made a central topic there. The issue of European unification movements and the corresponding institutions is not explicitly stated, but is at the most referred to in combination under "Current Issues". The Central Swiss syllabus, relevant for Lucerne, contains a joint subject History/Politics for the 7th to 9th school years. Here, the part taken up by History clearly predominates. Provided for as political themes in the 7th school year is the topic "Community – the cell of the State"; in the 8th school year "Functioning of the State". The syllabus contains for the 9th school year a few comments on the European unification processes.

The teaching materials are either prescribed by the respective canton or the choice of between two or three alternatives is enabled. Besides, teachers may include recommended teaching materials. These have included since 2007 for the *Primarstufe* (primary school) – as for the *Oberstufe* (intermediate, seventh to ninth

---

1   In German: Realschule, Sekundarschule and Bezirksschule.
2   Langzeitgymnasium.

grade) – the handout *"Politik und Demokratie – leben und lernen /* Politics and Democracy – living and learning" (Gollob et al., 2007).

In view of the fact that Civic Education as such but also the European unification movements and the development of European institutions are given sufficient coverage neither in the syllabuses nor in the teaching materials, the participation of teaching personnel in a project on Europe and knowledge of the EU signalizes a special motivation. Furthermore, on account of the marginal importance given to the topics, it could not be expected that the knowledge of Europe ascertained in the pre-test was to be found in a satisfactory way with the students. Therefore much more exciting was the question of whether the WebQuest would open up the access to a topic rather unfamiliar to the Swiss young people, whether they were interested in it, and with the intervention would further develop this interest, and whether they can widen their knowledge, as pursued, on the EU.

3. Method

The intervention study: Data come from the TEESAEC intervention study in Switzerland which was carried out in the cantons of Lucerne and Aargau. A sample of 17 school classes participated in an instructional intervention about CO_2 emissions and environmental issues in the European Union. The teaching material was prepared by the TEESAEC consortium and distributed to the experimental group in the form of a computer-supported WebQuest whilst in the control group the teachers volunteered and taught four lessons with the same contents. Before and subsequent to the four-hour intervention, students had to answer a questionnaire assessing conceptual knowledge on the European Union, political attitudes and interest in politics. In both cantons, an interview study followed the post-test assessment. The results of this additional investigation are not given any consideration here; they will be published at a later date.[3]

Sample: A total of 18 classes took part in the project. Students who were absent from one of the tests were discarded from the analysis. This results in a sample size of $N = 296$ for Switzerland. Ten classes come from the canton of Aargau and eight classes from the canton of Lucerne. The distribution of the classes into the experimental or control condition and their proportions according to the type of school are shown in Table 1. Due to the heterogeneous school systems in the two cantons

3   We would like to thank our colleagues who worked together with us in the study: Gina Aschwanden, Yvonne Leimgruber, Corinne Wyss for their work with the interviewing and evaluating.

the classes were allocated into a generalized school type model with basic require-ments (secondary modern school level D and C), extended requirements (secondary school level B) and high requirements (district schools level A).

Table 1
Sample

School type	Experimental classes		Control classes		Total
	AG	LU	AG	LU	
Basic requirements		1	1	3	5
Extended require-ments	4	4[a]	2		10
High requirements	1[b]			2[b]	4

Notes [a]: In one case in the canton Lucerne, the teaching was carried out jointly in a class of the school type with high requirements and a class of the school type with extended requirements in the subject of Geography, within whose framework the study took place. Both classes are listed in this presenta-tion under the heading "Type of school with extended requirements". [b] In the case of the canton Aar-gau, three classes of the school type with high requirements (district schools – *Bezirksschule*) are in-volved. This type of school recruits partly students who are in other cantons assigned to type of schools with extended requirements. In respect of the following evaluations, these three classes were also assigned to the school type with extended requirements.

It is not hard to recognize that there turns out to be an imbalance with the propor-tion of the school type in the experimental- and control group. The experimental group is composed of 9 classes with extended requirements and 1 class with basis requirements. In contrast, the control group consists of 4 classes of the school type with extended requirements and 4 classes of the school type with basic require-ments. Also in view of gender distribution, both groups are not identical. The pro-portion of boys in the experimental group amounts to 57.6% and in the control group to 40.5%. The students were between 14- and 15-year-old.

4. Instruments and procedures used with the data analysis

A questionnaire was presented to the students before and after the intervention as-sessing knowledge and competences, political attitudes and interest.

Knowledge and Competences: The questionnaire included 53 multiple-choice items with four answer options each. All items were coded dichotomous (0 = incor-rect, 1 = correct). The identical test-items were used both in the pre-and post-test questionnaire. A unidimensional Rasch analysis was conducted on the basis of the German and Swiss data record (n = 798) using ConQuest Software. Analysis veri-fied scale unidimensionality. The sample mean and the standard deviation of the introductory test served as reference variables for the scaling of the pre- and the post-test-items. The average student performance was preset at 500 points and the standard deviation of the distribution of student performance was preset at 100, with a probability to solve the tasks of 0.65 being assumed.[4]

Political attitudes towards and interest in the EU; self-estimated knowledge of the EU: The interest in, the self-estimated knowledge of the EU and the attitude of the students towards the EU were ascertained in the pre- and post-test by means of single items with a five-point Likert scale answer format (1 = not at all, 5 = very much). The statistical characteristic values (M, SD) are reported upon in the results section.

The classroom climate in the history or geography lessons was ascertained in a post-test questionnaire by items as follows: "The teacher encourages us to talk about political issues on which there are different opinions". The scale "comprised six items on a four-point Likert scale (4 = is totally relevant; 1 = is not at all relevant). Construct validation turned out to be satisfactory [M = 1.95, SD = .51, α = .74, N = 296]."

Owing to the low number of classes in the Swiss sub-sample, one had to forego analytical methods such as multilevel analyses which take into account the fact that students are nested within classes and therefore may have had similar learning experiences. Thus features between classes may vary but within the classes more homogeneous features could be identified. Neglecting the multilevel data structure in educational settings leads to the underestimation of standard errors of the fixed errors that inflates the apparent significance of the estimates (Hox, 2002). The restrictions coming along with the small sample size should be kept in mind in interpreting the following results, meaning that significant results on the p-value lower than .05 but higher than .01 should not be overestimated.

5. Results

Attitudes and interest: To what extent do young people feel associated with their own town, their own country (Switzerland) and the EU before the intervention? The students state that they feel themselves associated most strongly with Switzerland (M = 3.23, SD = .75), followed by the association with their own town (M = 3.13, SD = .72). The association with Europe is, on average, featured as the weakest (M = 2.00, SD = .76). A univariate variance analysis was conducted to investigate school type and gender differences. In view of the association with one's own

---

4   We would like to thank Valentin Eck, Karlsruhe, for his work and Vera Husfeldt, PH FHNW, for her support in creating the Swiss data record.

town or rather with Switzerland, the results revealed no systematic differences. In respect of the association with Europe, differences in types of school are observable [F (3, 292) = 11.58, p < .01, eta = .04]. The association with the EU turns out to be higher in the type of school with basic requirements (M = 2.24, SD = .75) than in the type of school with extended requirements (M = 1.91, SD = .74).

Which views on Europe do the interviewed students have? Table 2 shows means and estimated between group variances from a standard fixed-effects ANOVA.

Table 2
Means and estimated between group variances of the attitudes towards the European Union in the type of school with basic requirements and in the type of school with extended requirements

Item wording	Basic requirements		Extended requirements		F-test estimates	
	M	SD	M	SD	F (3, 292)	η^2
The politics of the EU results in making me feeling better.	2.30	0.76	2.12	0.75	3.34 ns	.01
The bigger countries benefit mostly from the EU.	2.95	0.66	2.73	0.73	5.70*	.02
The poorer countries benefit mostly from the EU.	2.53	0.83	2.48	0.82	0.30 ns	.00
A good EU citizen informs himself/herself on the standpoints of the parties before voting in an election.	3.01	0.69	3.24	0.69	6.46**	.02
A good EU citizen can give arguments why he/she is for or against a certain EU political policy.	3.00	0.75	3.27	0.70	8.17**	.03

Notes: 4-point Likert scale 1 = rejection, 4 = approval *p < .05, **p < .01, ***p<.000.

Of the five items relating to estimations of the EU, the first three items pick out as a central theme idea that the individual or states benefit from the EU. The last two relate in contrast rather to the idea that a citizen is indebted to the EU. The results show that the young people agree particularly with the last two items and they tend to think that the bigger countries benefit the most from the EU. The answering behaviour of the young people on these three items differs according to the types of school. The students of the type of school with extended requirements clearly agree more strongly with obligations of being a good European citizen. However, it remains unclear whether the idea of an obligation is accepted or the idea of a rationally and argumentatively supported politics is the leading thought.

Comparing the average answers of the boys and girls to these attitudes items, gender differences remain insignificant with one exception: There exists a single sex difference with the answering of item 4 (getting informed before the election), with the boys agreeing with this item, on average, less strongly than the girls [M_{boys} = 3.07, SD = .75; M $_{girls}$ = 3.28, SD = .62; F (3, 292) = 3.87, p <. 05, η^2 = .01].

The young people were questioned on their interest in politics in Switzerland (M = 2.42, SD = .91) and in the EU (M = 2.27, SD = .94) as well as on their knowledge of the EU (M = 2.18, SD = .81). Their answers lie exclusively beyond the average of the five-point Likert scale, namely between 2 and 3. Significant differences across the school types are observed regarding the interest in politics of the EU and the self-estimated knowledge of the EU (see Table 3). Students in the type of school with basic requirements estimate their interest in and their knowledge of the EU higher than those in the type of school with extended requirements. Boys and girls differ significantly in their self-estimated knowledge of the EU. The boys estimate their knowledge clearly higher than the girls [M_{boys} = 2.32, SD = .84; M_{girls} = 2.04, SD = .76; F (3, 292) = 4.55, p <. 05, η^2 = .02].

Table 3
Means and estimated between group variances on the average interest in politics in Switzerland and in the EU, knowledge of the EU in the type of school with basic requirements and in the type of school with extended requirements

	Basis requirements		Extended requirements		F-test estimates	
	M	SD	M	SD	F-test (3, 295)	η^2
Interest in Swiss politics	2.37	.87	2.43	.92	.32 n.s.	.00
Interest in European Union	2.54	1.09	2.17	.87	9.08*	.03
Self-estimated knowledge of the European Union	2.42	.76	2.09	.82	10.22*	.03

Notes: 5-point Likert scale, 1 = rejection, 5 = approval. *p < .05, **p < .01, ***p<.000.

The present results contrast with the IEA study for older youths (16- to 19-year-olds), according to which these have a negative identification with their own nation and, with this item, even range internationally at the lower end (Biedermann, 2005, and 2004, p. 20). The youths investigated here identify themselves with Europe clearly less than with their town or their country, what concurs with the study by Stamm (2007, p. 388). The reported differences from the types of school contrast insofar with the findings of Stamm (2007, p. 388ff.), as in her study the students of the type of school with high requirements feel themselves more associated with Europe than those in the type of school with basic requirements.

The finding that the identification with one's own country was given the highest estimation is perhaps determined by the fact that the association with one's own country was asked about in comparison to Europe. This might be the reason why Switzerland scored better than Europe.

6. Changes in the interest and in the knowledge between the pre-test and post-test depending on the chosen intervention setting

Does the interest in Swiss politics as well as the interest in the EU change between the pre-and post-test depending on the chosen intervention setting (experimental group vs. control group)? Figure 1 shows that in the pre-test questioning the average interest in politics in the control group was higher than in the experimental group ($t_{interest\ in\ politics\ at\ pre-test}$ = 2.18, df = 288, p < .05). In both groups, a slight increase of interest could be detected after the intervention. We thus carried out a two-factor repeated measures ANOVA with time as a within-subjects and group (type of intervention) as a between-subjects variable. The within-subject tests indicated a significant time effect, meaning that the interest development ascertained is statistically significant [F (1, 294) = 7.26, p < .01, η^2 = .02]. The type of the chosen intervention – WebQuest vs. traditional teaching in the control group – had no significant influence on the development of interest in politics.

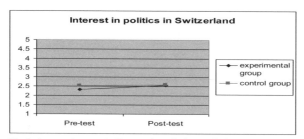

Fig. 1. Average interest in Swiss politics before and after the intervention

In respect of the average interest in the EU, the analyses result again in a higher value in the control group before the intervention, as shown in Figure 2. The group difference at the pre-test is significant ($t_{interest\ in\ the\ EU\ at\ pre-test}$ = 3.41, df = 278, p < .01). A slight but significant decrease in the interest in the EU is observed in both groups according to a two-factor repeated measures ANOVA [F (1, 294) = 9.95, p < .01, η^2 = .03]. The interaction effect between the time factor and the belonging to the experimental vs. control group turned out to be statistically insignificant, meaning that the type of intervention had hardly any influence on the development of interest in the EU. This result contradicts the assessment of Manzel saying that students showed a higher interest in politics following a WebQuest intervention on the topic of Europe (Manzel, 2007, p. 253).

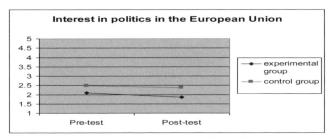

Fig. 2. Average interest in the European Union before and after the intervention

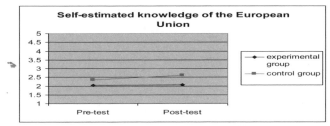

Fig. 3. Average self-estimated knowledge of the EU before and after the intervention

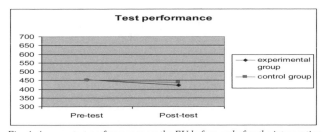

Fig. 4. Average test performances on the EU before and after the intervention

Figure 3 depicts the mean values of the experimental and control groups in respect of the self-estimated knowledge of the EU before and after the intervention. It shows that the experimental group started with a lower level of self-estimated knowledge than the control group ($t_{self\ estimated\ knowledge\ at\ pre-test}$ = 3.45, df = 283, p<.01). The self-estimation of one's own knowledge changes significantly between the pre- and the post-test [F (1, 294) = 9.14, p < .01, η^2 = .03]. Belonging to the control group goes along with a stronger increase in knowledge than the experimental group [F (1, 294) = 6.35, p < .05, η^2 = .02]. However, these findings should not be overestimated as the effect sizes (η^2) are pretty small.

Table 4
Influence of background variables, school type, the WebQuest participation and class-room climate on the development in interest, on the increase in self-estimated knowledge and on performance development

	Interest in Swiss politics t2	Interest in EU t2	Self-estimated know-ledge of EU t2	Post-Test perfor-mance
	β	β	β	β
Interest in Swiss politics t1	.53***			
Interest in EU t1		.49***		
Self-estimated knowledge of EU t1			.41***	
Pre-test performance				.84***
Type of school[a]	-.01	-.16**	-.12*	.01
Sex[b]	-.10 ^{t}	-.06	.05	.09**
Origin[c]				
at least one parent EU	-.09	-.07	-.03	-.06
at least one parent from outside EU	-.06	-.03	-.02	-.00
Language spoken at home[d]	.02	.02	-.01	.00
SES[e]	.10 ^{t}	-.02	-.00	-.03
Participation WebQuest[f]	-.01	-.13*	-.24***	-.07*
Classroom climate	.09	.10 ^{t}	.13**	.05 ^{t}
R^2	.33	.36	.33	.79

Notes: [a] basic requirement = 0, extended requirement = 1; [b] boy = 0, girl = 1; [c] both parents Swiss = 0, at least one parent EU = 1, at lest one parent from outside EU; [d] German = 0, other = 1; [e] SES = Socio-cultural background of family, [f] traditional teaching = 0, participation in WebQuest = 1; R^2 = explained variance; p < .05*, p < .01**, p < .000***

What about the test performances of the Swiss youths in respect of the EU displayed in Figure 4? The average knowledge of the Swiss youths lies clearly under the sample average of 500, which was stipulated jointly for the German and Swiss data record. This means that the knowledge of the Swiss youths on the EU turns out to be below-average. No performance differences are observed between the experimental group and the control group in the pre-test questionnaire. Furthermore, the two-factor repeated measures ANOVA revealed a significant reduction in knowledge between the pre- and post-test [F (1, 294) = 35.81, p < .000, η^2 = .11]. Moreover, the experimental- and the control group differ significantly in their development, for the drop in performance in the experimental group proves to be higher [F $(1, 294) = 6.47$, p $< .01$, $\eta^2 = .02$].

In a next step, several regression analyses were carried out including students background variables, school type, intervention type and classroom climate as predictor variables. By inserting respective input characteristics into the analyses, statements on the explanation of the development in interest or on the increase in knowledge can be made. This allows us to draw a more detailed picture about possible influencing factors on the interest and performance development.

Generally, it is shown that the input characteristics ascertained in the pre-test relative to the same characteristics in the post-test are highly predictive; that means, the interest in Swiss politics, the interest in the EU and the self-estimated knowledge of the EU remain relatively stable. In respect of the prediction on the development of interest in Swiss politics, no further characteristic proves to be significant. Changes in the interest in the EU and in the estimation of the increase in knowledge of the EU are influenced through the belonging to the school type. Thus the participation in the WebQuest has a negative effect on the development of both criteria. The individually perceived classroom climate plays a significant role in the development of the self-estimated knowledge. The test performance after the intervention turns out to be influenced to a strong degree by the foreknowledge measured in the pre-test. Girls set a stronger pace in the test performances than boys.

7. Discussion and outlook

From the results of the Swiss data, the EU appears to be a topic that young people are little affected by, have modest interest in, and know less about than their German counterparts. In this sense, the data reflect the institutional pre-conditions and corroborate the hitherto literature (even though with certain afore-mentioned deviations as per the Stamm study, 2007).

With a look at the changes that were expected from the intervention, the following points can be formulated: the participation in the WebQuest (experimental group) leads to negative effects on the attitudes of the students (interest, self-estimated knowledge) as well as in the test performance. Especially the result that the interest of the students has a negative development should be critically considered. Following the interest theory (Krapp, 1998), which assumes that the interest experienced and felt in the learning situation constitutes an important prerequisite for to continue the preoccupation with the subject of interest – in the ideal case beyond the school – , the negative finding is worrying. According to the presented results the WebQuest employed does not meet the educational requirement that was originally formulated.

The fact that the markedness and development of the interest shows up more negatively with the experimental group than with the control group could therefore be affected by the unbalanced distribution of the type of schools in the experimental and control group setting. In fact, in the experimental group were clearly more classes from the school type with extended requirements. These are seen to be clearly less interested in the EU (contrary to the findings of Stamm, 2007) than the classes from the school type with basic requirements.

The results on the performance test (decrease in knowledge) contradicts the results of Manzel (2007, p. 241ff.), according to which classes that had worked with a WebQuest on European core concepts showed a higher level of knowledge of European politics after the intervention. But also, the control group that had worked without a WebQuest on the European material, expierienced with Manzel (2007, p. 241) an increase in knowledge; what in the present study was not the case. This finding is still noteworthy, even though for the present study it must be acknowledged that the sample is not representative.

The changes in knowledge that come to light cannot therefore be further indicated in content. They reflect presumably to a larger extent test acceptance. The drop in test scores is most preferably explainable by the test fatigue of the students.

One must consider that a basic assumption on the acquisition of knowledge, which forms the basis for the conceptualization of this project, has to be rejected as not confirmed given the present results. This assumption comprises that the involvement of young people with the WebQuest results in the fact that not alone simple working knowledge but conceptual knowledge is developed, which is available within the framework of other topics. The present data lets no conclusion be drawn whether such a conceptual knowledge was developed. It cannot therefore be further explored why a possibly acquired conceptual knowledge does not make its mark in the post-test within the meaning of an increase in knowledge. On the one hand, it is possible that little new information was learned; but on the other hand, it is also conceivable that the knowledge acquired by the young people in the post-test cannot be called upon. In the second case, an "inert knowledge" would be involved (Renkl, 1996). Whether acquired knowledge is of effective use for thinking and recognition in other contexts, depends on the interplay of individual and situative factors; inter alia upon getting to grips with the contents in diverse application and problem situations. It remains to be investigated to what extent the WebQuest setting used holds such learning experiences ready.

References

Amadeo, J.-A., Torney-Purta, J., Lehmann, R., Husfeldt, V. & Nikolova, R. (2002). *Civic Knowledge and Engagement: An IEA Study of Upper Secondary Students in Sixteen Countries.* Amsterdam: The International Association for the Evaluation of Educational Achievement.

Biedermann, H. (2004). *Werden junge Menschen auf ihre Rollen als Staatsbürgerinnen und Staatsbürger genügend vorbereitet? Ergebnisse der IEA-Studie. Civic Education II (16-19-Jährige)* unveröff. Vortragsmanuskript. Fribourg.

Biedermann, H. (2005). *Demokratiepädagogik und Politische Bildung in der Schweiz – eine bildungspolitische Grundlage.* Unveröff. Vortragsmanuskript. Berlin.

Biedermann, H. (2006). *Junge Menschen an der Schwelle politischer Mündigkeit. Partizipation: Patentrezept politischer Identitätsfindung?* Münster: Waxmann.

Biedermann, H. (2007). Quantitative Sozialforschung zur Politischen Bildung. In D. Lange & V. Reinhardt (Eds.). *Basiswissen Politische Bildung* (Band 4, p. 28−38). Baltmannsweiler: Schneider Verlag Hohengehren.

Bieri Buschor, C. & Forrer, E. (2005). *Cool, kompetent und kein bisschen weise? Überfachliche Kompetenzen junger Erwachsener am Übergang zwischen Schule und Beruf.* Eidgenössische Jugend- und Rekrutenbefragungen ch-x. Wissenschaftliche Reihe 18. Zürich: Rüegger.

Gollob, R. et al. (Eds.) (2007). *Politik und Demokratie – leben und lernen.* Bern: schulverlag.

Hox, J. (2002). *Multilevel Analysis. Techniques and Applications.* London: Lawrence Erlbaum Associates.

Krapp, A. (1998). Entwicklung und Förderung von Interessen im Unterricht. In *Psychologie in Erziehung und Unterricht, 45,* 186−203.

Manzel, S. (2007). *Kompetenzzuwachs im Politikunterricht. Ergebnisse einer Interventionsstudie zum Kernkonzept Europa.* Münster: Waxmann.

Oser, F. & Biedermann, H. (2003). *Jugend ohne Politik: Ergebnisse der IEA Studie zu politischem Wissen, Demokratieverständnis und gesellschaftlichem Engagement von Jugendlichen in der Schweiz im Vergleich mit 27 anderen Ländern.* Zürich: Rüegger.

Oser, F., Steinmann, S., Maiello, C., Quesel, C. & Villiger, C. (2005). *Zur Entwicklung der politischen Kognitionen: Schlussbericht* (Universität Fribourg). Freiburg (CH).

Renkl, A. (1996). Träges Wissen: Wenn Erlerntes nicht genutzt wird. In *Psychologische Rundschau, 47,* 78−92.

Stamm, M. (2007). Jugendliche in der Schweiz und ihr Blick nach Europa. Ausgewählte Ergebnisse einer Schweizer Langzeitstudie. In H. Biedermann, F. Oser & C. Quesel, *Vom Gelingen und Scheitern Politischer Bildung. Studien und Entwürfe* (p. 383−398). Zürich/Chur: Rüegger.

Torney-Purta, J., Lehmann, R., Oswald, H. & Schulz, W. (2001). *Citizenship and Education in Twenty-eight Countries: Civic Knowledge and Engagement at Age Fourteen.* Amsterdam: International Association for the Evaluation of Educational Achievement.

Knowledge about the European Union among Dutch youth: levels, origins, and what secondary school education contributes

Sanne A.M. Rijkhoff & Henk Dekker

1. Introduction

What are the main predictors of the level of knowledge about the European Union among young people in the Netherlands? What does secondary school education about the Union contribute to this? These are the intriguing questions that we want to answer in this contribution, presenting the findings from our analyses of data from 204 Dutch secondary school students.

It is important to study knowledge about the European Union because this is an important ingredient of European and democratic citizenship competence (Popkin and Dimock, 1999; Milner, 2002), and because of its effects on other orientations and behavior with respect to the EU. Knowledge affects the content of beliefs, o-pinions, preferences, attitudes, behavioral intentions, and behavior. Knowledge helps citizens understand their own interests and has a positive effect on the decision to go and vote at elections (Popkin & Dimock, 2000; O'Toole et al., 2003). The referendum about the Treaty establishing a Constitution for Europe held on 1 June 2005 in the Netherlands offers a clear example of the relevance of political knowledge for political behavior and orientations. Data from the post-referendum Flash Eurobarometer 172 (European Commission, 2005) show that most abstainers indicated that they believed they had not been sufficiently informed on the Constitution to go and vote (51%). Asked for their reasons to vote 'No', most voters again indicated the lack of information as the main reason (32%).

It is also important to study knowledge among young people because there is growing research-based evidence that knowledge acquired during the mid- to late teen years has an effect on knowledge later in life (Sears, 2003). Political knowledge at time2 is strongly influenced by the level of knowledge at time1 (Cassel and Lo, 1997). This emphasizes the importance of learning about the European Union at an early age (see also Galston, 2001).

Formal education about the European Union is important to study because the school is the only socialization agent that reaches all young citizens. If we want all young citizens to be informed about the European Union, the school should offer effective education on the subject. Research into the effects of general political education in schools has shown mixed results. It is not self-evident that lessons about the European Union are effective and always contribute to an increase in knowledge.

2. The concept of knowledge

In general, two different kinds of knowledge are distinguished: subjective and objective knowledge. Subjective knowledge is self-assessed knowledge, i.e., the self-perception that one has no, a little, or much knowledge. Sometimes researchers use subjective knowledge as a surrogate for objective knowledge to avoid the difficulties relating to measuring objective knowledge (Mondak, 2001). However, congruence among the two types is not self-evident; someone may believe to know a lot but fail the test. Therefore we focus on objective, i.e., demonstrated, knowledge. People have objective knowledge if they are able to answer correctly a number of informative and insight questions about an object without aid or assistance.

Knowledge is to be distinguished from other cognitions — such as beliefs – and from opinions, attitudes, emotions, values, behavioral intentions, and behavior. The difference between knowledge and beliefs is especially important. A belief is something that is believed to be a fact but cannot be proven to be actually 'true', for instance because data are missing or the concept has more than one meaning. Knowledge is restricted to 'the truth', i.e., what has been or can be proven to be 'true'.

Three levels of knowledge are distinguished (Bloom et al., 1956). Low-level knowledge includes memorization and reproduction. The subject is able to answer correctly a number of simple informative questions about an object without any aid or assistance thanks to remembering a particular bit or bits of information stored in the long-term memory. Middle-level knowledge includes insight or understanding and demands interpreting information and solving problems that have just one correct solution. High-level knowledge includes solving problems that theoretically have more than one correct solution. This expert knowledge cannot realistically be expected among 'ordinary' citizens. Most studies of knowledge about the European Union focus on low-level knowledge; the dependent variable in this study is middle-level knowledge.

Another distinction is that between concrete and theoretical knowledge. Concrete knowledge includes knowledge of specific objects (EU, Council of Ministers, Commission, European Parliament, etc.). Theoretical knowledge includes knowledge of concepts, conceptual structures, models, and theories. Most studies of European Union knowledge focus on concrete knowledge; in this study both concrete and theoretical knowledge were analyzed.

European Union knowledge can not be equated with knowledge about national politics. Knowledge about the European Union seems to be structurally distinct from knowledge about national politics (Delli Carpini & Keeter, 1993). A cumulative effect, however, may be expected; people with much international political knowledge probably also have much national political knowledge.

The European Union has various dimensions, but here we focus on the political dimension. This dimension includes polity (i.e., the political system, including political structures and institutions), politics (i.e., political processes, political events, and political actors), and policies (including political issues and programs).

Empirical studies usually find a low level of political knowledge. Students, although literate enough, still show political ignorance (Dekker & Portengen, 2000; Torney-Purta et al., 2001). For many people politics is *'terra incognita'*. Democracies are 'don't know democracies' (Lister, 1976). There is no evidence that overall levels of political knowledge have altered much over time (Delli Carpini & Keeter, 1991 and 1996; Galston, 2001). Is this also true for the knowledge about the European Union?

3. Variances in knowledge: possible explanations

We see three categories of possible explanations for variance in the knowledge about the European Union: the ability to absorb and process information about the European Union, the motivation to do so, and opportunities to receive this information directly, through one's own experiences, and/or indirectly through socialization and education (Dekker & Nuus, 2007).

The first category includes cognitive ability. Testing all elements of cognitive ability requires a battery of questions, including intelligence test scores (IQ), which are almost impossible to include in a political science study. In the few political knowledge studies conducted in the past, surrogate measures such as level of education and/or school achievement, were used as it is generally accepted that IQ and these school variables are closely related. We hypothesize that the higher the level of education, the more knowledge about the European Union someone will have.

The second category of possible explanations for variance in knowledge about the European Union is the different motivations to absorb and process information about the EU. The motivation for learning is important because of humans' limited cognitive abilities, the economical functioning of the brain, and the complex nature of politics. Possible motivations are attachment to, attitude towards, positive emotion with respect to and interest in the European Union. Other possible motivations are the intention to vote for the European Parliament, and the conviction that to be sufficiently informed is part of good EU citizenship.

Personal attachment to one's own city or town, country, or continent, as well as positive attitudes and positive emotions form motivational forces for political learning. In the case of a distant object such as the European Union is we may expect that positive emotions will make it attractive to learn more about that object (Marcus, 2003). We hypothesize that the greater someone's attachment to the European Union, positive attitudes towards the European Union, and positive emotions with respect to the European Union, the more knowledge about the European Union someone will have.

What also drives (voluntary) political learning is interest (Cassel & Lo, 1997; Dekker & Portengen, 2000; Larcinese, 2005). People who are interested expect that knowing more will result in positive feelings, for example pleasure, satisfaction of curiosity, and a stronger feeling of identity. We hypothesize that the greater people's interest in the European Union, the greater their political knowledge will be.

Another motivational force for learning may be positive behavioral intentions. An important behavioral intention with respect to the European Union is the intention to vote at European Parliament elections. Once people have developed the intention to go and vote at the European Parliament elections (for instance because they consider voting a civic duty or part of good citizenship, or relevant others are trying to convince them to go and vote) they may be motivated to know more about the elections, the body to be elected, the parties and their candidates, and current issues. We hypothesize that the stronger someone's intention to go and vote for the European Parliament, the greater their knowledge about the European Union will be.

The third category of possible explanations for variance in knowledge about the European Union includes the opportunities to receive information about the European Union either directly, through one's own experiences, and/or indirectly through socialization. Because most people do not have the opportunity to participate in European Union politics, not many will have an experiential knowledge about the Union. What European knowledge people do have must for the larger part have come from socialization. Most people probably acquire European knowledge mainly by receiving and accepting information from relevant others, i.e., if their political socialization includes receiving information about the European Union. This may for instance come from parents, school, mass media, friends, social networks, politicians and political organizations, and public relations offices of the European Union (Dekker, 1991 and 1994; Muxel, 2001; Hahn, 1998; Farnen et al., 2000 and 2005). We assume that the family is the most important socialization agency for our young research population. We hypothesize that the higher the parents' political literacy, the more knowledge about the European Union the child will have. The group of peers and friends in particular is expected to be another important socialization agency. We hypothesize that greater activity in a youth club or organization will mean more knowledge about the European Union. Finally, politicians and political organizations may also be expected to be important socializers. We hypothesize that the more active someone is in a political organization, the more knowledge about the European Union one will have.

Gender is a background variable in our analysis. In general, boys/men are more knowledgeable on politics than girls/women. However, gender as such does not say much; important variables linked to sex/gender are personal characteristics such as political experiences or the lack of them, and political and politically relevant gender socialization (Dow 2009).

4. Data collection

In order to test these hypotheses we conducted a survey among Dutch youth, using the questionnaire developed jointly by the six partners in the 'Teacher Empowerment to Educate Students to Become Active European Citizens' project. For more information about this project we refer to the contribution of Weisseno and Eck in this volume.

Respondents filled out the standardized questionnaire containing 65 single- and multi-item questions, covering knowledge about the European Union and all the explanatory variables mentioned in our hypotheses. The complete version of the questionnaire is available from the authors on request. The data were collected between January and April 2009, during regular school hours of 50 minutes.

In total, 204 students from nine classes in three schools filled out the questionnaire. We targeted the age group of 16-year olds. The two levels of (higher) secondary education represented in the sample are higher general education ('havo': six classes) and pre-university education ('vwo': three classes). Our project aims not only to analyze existing knowledge but also to study the effects of a new teaching and learning project for secondary-school students and teachers.

5. European Union knowledge

Knowledge about the European Union – the dependent variable – was measured by 53 standard multiple-choice questions with four answer options including one correct answer. An example: 'The European Union wants to regulate alcohol advertising. The European Parliament agrees, but the Council of Ministers rejects the proposal. What happens as a result?' The answer options are: 'The regulation does not apply', 'The regulation applies if 70% or more of the MEP's vote in favor', 'The regulation applies if the President of the European Commission agrees', and 'The regulation applies only in those member states that agree to it'.

The knowledge questions covered all three fields of 'the political': polity, politics and policy. The 24 polity questions related to the European Commission (eight questions), Council of Ministers (eight), and the European Parliament (eight). The 10 politics questions related to internal politics, including decision making in Council and Commission (seven questions) and external politics (three questions). The 19 policy questions related to policies with respect to peace (two questions), economic prosperity (one), internal market (one), environment (two), equal rights (two), consumer protection (one), fishery, poultry (three), free trade (one), external relations (one), energy (one) and immigration (four).

The average number of correct answers in the test was 28, which indicates that for the majority of respondents the test was not too simple or too difficult. Eight questions were relatively simple (receiving > 70% correct answers) while five questions were relatively difficult (< 30% correct answers).

More than four out of ten students have considerable or very considerable knowledge (> 30 correct answers: 43%), while one third has average knowledge (22 to 30 correct answers; 32%), and about a quarter of the respondents has no, very little, or little political knowledge (< 22 correct answers; 25%). In order to measure these levels we simply counted the correct answers. The index runs from 0 (= all answers are wrong) to 53 (= all answers are correct). This way of counting was possible since the answers to the 53 questions formed a reliable index (Cronbach's alpha = .847, N= 204). Table 1 shows the percentages of the respondents with very considerable, considerable, average, little, very little or no European Union knowledge.

We also measured subjective knowledge in order to find the correlation between what is shown in the knowledge test result and the way respondents themselves perceive their knowledge. The question was worded as follows: „On a scale from 1 to 5, how much do you know about the European Union, where 1 means „I know nothing at all" and 5 means „I know very much"? If respondents perceived their knowledge correctly the simple question 'How much do you know about the European Union' would suffice in the follow-up analysis. However, we found that objective knowledge and subjective knowledge did not correlate (Somers' d = -.02, N = 203). Clearly, in our dataset objective and subjective knowledge are two different variables; a simple subjective knowledge question is not a valid measurement of objective knowledge.

We also asked the respondents whether or not they wanted to improve their knowledge about the European Union. The respondents were given four answer options to choose from. A majority wanted more knowledge: one third of the total agreed with 'I want to have more information about the European Union' (36%) and two out of ten agreed with 'I need to get more knowledge about the European Union' (21%). Almost two out of ten answered 'I am satisfied with the knowledge I have about the European Union' (17%). A relatively large group do not know (26%).

Table 1

European Union knowledge among our sample of Dutch secondary school students in 2009

	Correct answers	%
Very considerable knowledge	43–53	2 (4)
Considerable knowledge	31–42	41 (84)
Average knowledge	22–30	32 (66)
Little knowledge	10–21	25 (50)
Very little or no knowledge	00–09	0 (0)

Note: Scores are percentages, exact numbers are given in parentheses, $N = 204$

6. European Union knowledge predictors

The independent variables in our analysis were: attachment to the European Union, the attitude towards the European Union, emotion with respect to the European Union, interest in the European Union, intention to vote for the European Parliament, considering knowledge part of good EU citizenship, and political socialization at home and in youth and/or political organizations.

Attachment to the European Union was measured by the following question: 'You can have different feelings of attachment with respect to your village, town or city, with respect to your country, and with respect to the European Union, namely very strong, fairly strong, not strong, not at all. How strongly do you feel attached to ...'. Only about two out of ten respondents feel very or fairly strongly attached to the European Union (22%), while six out of ten feel weakly attached to the EU (59%) and two out of ten do not feel attached to the European Union at all (19%). Much more respondents feel very or fairly strongly attached to their own country and town or city (82% and 80%, respectively).

Students' attitude towards the European Union was measured by three questions. The first question asked about attitude directly: 'What is your attitude towards the European Union? Half of the respondents were 'neutral' (50%). From the other half, almost four out of ten were positive ('very positive': 9%, 'positive': 27%), while a small minority were negative ('negative': 5%, 'very negative': 1%) and one out of ten answered 'do not know' (10%). The second question was: 'Generally speaking, do you think that the Netherlands' membership of the European Union is a good thing/ bad thing/ neither good nor bad/ don't know?' The majority thought membership of the European Union is a good thing (61%), while only a small number of students considered membership a bad thing (7%), 16% answered 'neither good nor bad', and around one out of ten did not know (12%). The third question was: 'Taking everything into consideration, would you say that the Netherlands have on balance benefited or not from being a member of the European Union?' More than half of our sample of students answered 'benefited' (63%), while small minorities answered „not benefited" (12%) or did not know (12%). The latter two questions had been taken from the Eurobarometer (Commission 2001, 2008, 2009). The three questions formed a scale with a low reliability (Cronbach's alpha = .57, N = 196); only the first, direct, question was included in our further analysis.

Positive emotion with respect to the European Union was measured by asking the respondents to react to the following statement: 'EU policies make me feel positive'. More respondents agreed with the statement ('Agree completely': 5%, 'tend to agree': 64%) than disagreed ('Tend not to agree': 28%, 'do not agree at all': 3%).

Interest in the European Union was measured by the following question: 'On a scale of 1 to 5: How interested are you in the European Union?' Respondents indicated their self-assessed level of interest by putting a cross in one of the five squares on a line. Options ranged from 'Not at all' to 'Very interested'. More than seven out of ten respondents were not or not at all interested in the European Union (51% and 23%, respectively). Two out of ten were partly interested (21%). A very small minority were interested or very much interested (3% and 3%, respectively). There is somewhat more interest in Dutch politics, which we measured in the same way, although still not very high (no and not at all interested 52%, partly interested 30%, and interested and very much interested 14% and 3%, respectively.

The intention to vote for the European Parliament was measured by the following question: 'Imagine, tomorrow an election of the European Parliament will be held and you are eligible to vote. Will you certainly go and vote, probably go, probably not go, or certainly not go?' Less than two out of ten would certainly go (18%) and about one third would probably go and vote (35%). Three out of ten would probably not go (31%) and less than two out of ten would certainly not go and vote (17%).

Whether or not knowledge was considered part of good EU citizenship was measured by asking the respondents to react to two statements. The first was: 'Good EU citizens know what the various political parties think about the EU before they go and vote'. A clear majority agreed or completely agreed with this statement (71%), while three out of ten respondents disagreed or completely disagreed (29%). The second statement was: 'A good EU citizen can give arguments why he is pro or contra a decision of the EU'. A clear majority again agreed or completely agreed with this statement (78%), while two out of ten disagreed or completely disagreed (22%). The two items formed a reliable scale (Cronbach's alpha = .72; $N = 203$).

The socialization variables regard the family, and youth and political organizations. Since a direct test of parents' political literacy was not possible, we used the surrogate variable of the number of books at home as perceived by the respondents. The question was worded as follows: 'How many books are there in your home? There are usually about 40 books per meter of shelving. Do not count magazines, newspapers, or your school books'. Six answer options were available, varying from '0-10 books' to 'More than 500 books'. One out of ten respondents indicated 0-10 books (10%), slightly more students indicated 11-25 books (14%). A quarter of the students indicated 26-100 (25%), whereas an equal number of respondents, namely two out of ten, indicated 101-200 or 201-500 books (19%). Finallye, less than two out of ten students indicated they had more than 500 books at home (14%).

The question regarding youth and/or political organizations was worded as follows: 'Do you play an active part in any of the following organizations?', the organizations being 'Youth group or youth organization' and 'Political organization, e.g. political party, environmental protection organization, protection of animals organization, migrant organization or social organization'. The two answer options were 'Yes' or 'No'. One out of ten students indicated they were active in a youth organization (11%), while the majority of the students were not active (89%). An even larger majority of the students were not (active) members of a political organization (98%).

Table 2 presents the correlations between knowledge about the European Union and the various independent variables. There is one, though weak correlation: the correlation between European Union knowledge and political socialization in the family (Somers' $d = .22$, $p < .001$, $N = 204$). The correlations with all other independent variables are non-significant.

Table 2
European Union knowledge correlations

	Somer's d	Pearson's r
Cognitive ability		
Education level	.15	.11
Motivations		
Attachment to the EU	.03	.01
Positive emotion with respect to the EU	.11	.11
Attitude towards the EU[+]	.04	.01
Interest in the EU	.07	.04
Intention to vote for European Parliament[+]	.02	.01
Considering knowledge part of good EU citizenship	-.02	.03
Opportunities		
Political socialization at home, number of books	.24**	.29**
Membership youth organization	-.10	-.06
Membership political organization	-.04	-.00
Background variables		
Gender	.10	.10
Age	-.07	-.08

Note: Scores are correlations with knowledge as dependent variable. $N = 204$, [+] $N= 197$, * $p < .05$; ** $p < .001$

Table 3 presents the multiple regression coefficients with European Union knowledge. Political socialization in the family is also the variable with most predictive power for EU knowledge, controlled for the impact of the other variables. When there are more books available at home, the level of knowledge about the EU increases by almost 2 points (two additional questions answered correctly). Two variables are almost significant: educational level, and positive emotion with respect to the EU. Educational level was measured in two categories ('havo' and 'vwo'). The results of the regression analysis show that when we take students at a higher educational level into account the scores on European Union knowledge increase by slightly more than 2 points. This result is not surprising, since students at a higher level generally have a higher IQ and learn more easily than students at a lower level. Positive emotion with respect to the EU was measured by one variable, ranging from 0-6. However, if students have more positive emotions with respect to the EU their knowl-edge scores increase by approximately 2 points. The percentage of variance in knowledge about the European Union by all the independent variables together is a relatively low 8%.

Table 3
European Union knowledge predictors

	B	β	t	p
Education level	2.40	.13	1.79	.08
Attachment to the EU	-.55	-.05	-.53	.60
Positive emotion with respect to the EU	2.01	.14	1.72	.09
Attitude towards the EU[+]	-.34	-.03	-.38	.71
Interest in the EU	-.11	-.01	-.13	.90
Intention to vote for European Parliament[+]	-.39	-.05	-.59	.56
Considering knowledge part of good EU citizenship	.53	.04	.58	.56
Political socialization at home, number of books	1.69	.31	4.05	.00
Membership youth organization	-1.89	-.07	-.94	.35
Membership political organization	-.77	-.01	-.19	.85
Gender	1.87	.11	1.50	.14
Age	-.61	-.06	-.78	.44
R^2	.14			
R^2 (adjusted)	.08			

Note: Linear regression analysis, missing values excluded pairwise, $N = 203$, [+] $N = 197$.

7. European knowledge and education

In this section we analyze the data for the 40 students who participated in an innovative web-based series of lessons about the European Union and a control group of 33 students from the same grade and school, in order to find out what the web lessons contribute to the students' European Union knowledge. These 73 students are a subsample of the 204 students of the previous section. All students filled in the exact same questionnaire, but only the students in the subsample filled in the questionnaire twice.

We invited one of the schools whose students participated in the knowledge test presented in the previous section, to offer the new web-based series of lessons on the European Union to two classes and to offer a parallel series of lessons, using material of the teacher's own choosing, to two other classes from the same level of education and grade ('havo 4'), as a control group. In the WebQuest classes the students worked exclusively with online material and answered questions directly on the webpage. In the control classes teachers were free to choose their own methods of teaching and educational materials. All students completed a questionnaire twice, both before starting (pre-test) and after finishing (post-test) the lessons.

What is the impact of the web-based teaching and learning unit on students' understanding of the European Union? Does the use of WebQuest as a self-instructional tool result in a greater increase in knowledge than a purely teacher-controlled teaching environment? We hypothesize that students who use WebQuest develop more knowledge about the European Union than the students who enjoyed a series of lessons of a different type.

The new series of lessons – WebQuest – has been developed jointly by the six partners in the 'Teacher Empowerment to Educate Students to Become Active European Citizens' project. The aim of the lessons is to strengthen youngsters' political literacy with respect to the European Union in order for them to become well-informed, engaged, and active European citizens. The teaching method is characterized by the following key words: active, computer-assisted self-directed inquiry, and problem solving. The curriculum material, which is issue- rather than institution-oriented, includes the online WebQuest lessons for the students and a guide for teachers. For more information about the WebQuest lessons and the project, we refer to the chapter by Weisseno and Eck in this volume.

The 73 students in the experimental and control groups (the subsample) did not differ too much from 204 students together in the whole sample. The difference in knowledge between the whole sample and the pre-test knowledge of the subsample was not significant. The mean scores were 5.29 for the pre-test knowledge of the whole sample, and 5.26 for the pre-test knowledge of the subsample (scores on a 0-10 scale). The distribution among the five levels of knowledge at the pre-test was the same as that of the whole sample (very considerable, considerable, average, little, very little or no knowledge). The distribution over the same five levels at the post-test, from a high to a low level of knowledge, was 1%, 39%, 30%, 29%, and 1%, respectively. The knowledge indexes for both pre- and post-test were reliable (Cronbach's alphas are, respectively, .78 and .86, $N = 73$).

Table 4 presents the data for the two tests. Surprisingly, the post-test results showed lower mean scores on the 0-53 knowledge index than the pre-test scores. Post-test student scores were significantly lower than for the pre-test (t (72) = 4.62, $p < .001$, $d = .54$). The students in the Web-Quest group did worse on the post-test than on the pre-test (t (39) = 2.85, $p < .01$, $d = .45$), while the two scores for both times of the students in the control group did not significantly differ (t (32) = 1.65, $p = .11$). One could argue that the paired samples t-test could not be applied here because of dependence of observations due to the fact that students could have talked to each other between the two tests. However, it does not seem very likely that many students have exchanged and remembered the answers, since the test included a large number of questions of which quite a few were difficult and detailed.

Table 4
European Union knowledge: scores at pre- and post-test

		M	SD	Min	Max	N
PRE	WebQuest	28.53 (5.38)	7.03 (1.33)	12 (2.26)	42 (7.92)	40
	Control	27.09 (5.11)	7.10 (1.34)	12 (2.26)	37 (6.98)	33
	Total	27.88 (5.26)	7.05 (1.33)	12 (2.26)	42 (7.92)	73
POST	WebQuest	24.90 (4.70)	8.14 (1.54)	12 (2.26)	45 (8.49)	40
	Control	25.03 (4.73)	9.74 (1.84)	5 (.94)	39 (7.36)	33
	Total	24.96 (4.71)	8.83 (1.67)	5 (.94)	45 (8.49)	73

Note: Same school, 4 classes, same level of education ('havo 4'), knowledge index runs from 0-53, scores on index scale from 0-10 are given in parentheses.

Table 5
European Union knowledge predictors at the post-test

	B	β	t	p
European knowledge at pre-test	.75	.60	5.04	.00
Attachment to the EU	2.38	.18	1.22	.23
Positive emotion with respect to the EU	-1.64	-.09	-.65	.52
Attitude towards the EU[+]	-.28	-.04	-.33	.74
Interest in the EU	-1.49	-.14	-.86	.39
Intention to vote for European Parliament[+]	1.36	.15	1.23	.22
Considering knowledge part of good EU citizenship	-2.36	-.18	-1.58	.12
Political socialization at home: number of books	-.10	-.02	-.12	.91
Membership youth organization (reference category: no)	2.84	.12	1.06	.30
Membership political organization (reference category: no)	4.50	.08	.73	.47
Gender (reference category: male)	.72	.04	.32	.75
Age	-.06	-.01	-.04	.97
Teaching method (reference category: control)	-1.50	-.09	-.73	.47
R^2	.39			
R^2 (adjusted)	.25			

Note: Linear regression analysis, missing values excluded pairwise, $N = 73$, [+] $N = 70$. Membership of a youth or political organization is a dummy variable, with no = 0 and yes = 1. Gender was also a dummy variable with male = 0 and female = 1, and so was teaching method with control = 0 and Web-Quest = 1.

The 'good' news is that the percentage of students who were satisfied with their level of knowledge about the European Union increased considerably (pre-test: 21%, post-test: 38%), whereas the number of students who still want to know more about the European Union stayed almost the same (pre-test: 27%, post-test: 26%). Subjective knowledge about the European Union also changed: less students think that they know nothing or little about the European Union (scale value 1: 'I know nothing at all': pretest: 14%, post-test: 13%; scale value 2: little knowledge: pretest: 50%, post-test: 44%; scale value 3: pretest: 29%, post-test: 39%; scale value 4: pretest: 7%, post-test: 4%; scale value 5: 'I know very much': pretest: 0%, post-test: 0%).

The correlation analysis, including knowledge about the European Union at the post-test, the various independent variables, introduced in the previous sections, completed with knowledge about the European Union at the pre-test and teaching method, showed that the post-test knowledge correlates only with pre-test knowl-

Table 6
Differences in pre- and post-test questionnaire scores

		Pre	Post
Attachment to the EU	Quite close	9.7 (7)	17.8 (13)
	Very close	2.7 (2)	4.1 (3)
Feeling good about EU policy	Tend to agree	74.0 (54)	69.9 (51)
	Fully agree	1.4 (1)	2.7 (2)
Attitude towards the EU	Positive	24.7 (18)	23.3 (17)
	Very positive	8.2 (6)	4.1 (3)
Interest in EU	Somewhat	23.3 (17)	21.9 (16)
	Very much	1.4 (1)	5.5 (4)
Satisfied with knowledge about the EU		20.5 (15)	38.4 (28)
Wants more knowledge about the EU		27.4 (20)	26.0 (19)
Needs to know more about the EU		17.8 (13)	11.0 (8)
Intention to vote	Probably yes	26.0 (19)	26.0 (19)
	Certainly yes	16.4 (12)	19.2 (14)
Subjective knowledge:	Nothing at all	13.9 (10)	12.5 (9)
	2	50.0 (36)	44.4 (32)
	3	29.2 (21)	38.9 (28)
	4	6.9 (5)	4.2 (3)
	Very much	0 (0)	0 (0)

Note: Scores are percentages, exact numbers are given in parentheses

edge ($r = .55$, $p < 001$). The difference in teaching method – WebQuest or other – and all other independent variables do not significantly correlate with post-test knowledge.

Table 5 presents the multiple regression coefficients with European Union knowledge at the post-test. The difference in lessons is not a significant predictor of post-test knowledge either. The regression analysis shows that pre-test knowledge is the one and only significant predictor for the level of post-test knowledge.

Table 6 presents the pre- and post-test data with respect to the independent variables. More students in the post-test questionnaire indicated feeling attached to the EU (pre-test: 12%, post-test: 22%). Students were somewhat less positive about the EU after the lessons than before (pre-test: 33%, post-test: 27%). However, their interest in the EU slightly increased (pre-test: 25%, post-test: 27%). Feelings about EU policy and intention to vote for the European Parliament remained the same. However, a paired samples t-test indicated that none of these variables show significant differences in mean scores between the pre- and post-test answers.

8. Conclusion

What are the main predictors of middle-level concrete and theoretical European Union knowledge among young people in the Netherlands? The single most important predictor is parental socialization, measured by an indication of the number of books available at home. All other predictors, based on theory and previous research, do not seem to explain this knowledge about the EU.

These findings are surprising. It may be that our test, because of it specific question and answer format, measures not only knowledge about the EU but also advanced cognitive capacity.

What is the contribution of the newly developed WebQuest teaching material to students' knowledge about the EU? The WebQuest introduces the EU by means of a case study. This is a different approach than the usual institutional view ordinary textbooks bring. Moreover, the students worked autonomously in pairs, with the WebQuest provided on a computer. A control group of students received regular lessons about the EU. We found that for the level of knowledge about the EU tested after the lessons, the only significant predictor was the level of knowledge at the pre-test. Neither of the types of formal school education studied – WebQuest or other – resulted in higher scores on our test of concrete and conceptual knowledge about the European Union.

These findings are also surprising. It may be that the fit between the aims of the lessons, their content, and the test questions was not perfect. More research and development is necessary to arrive at effective education about the EU.

References

Bloom, B., Engelhardt, W., Hill, W., Furst, E. & Krathwohl, D. (Eds.) (1956). *Taxonomy of Educational Objectives Handbook 1: Cognitive Domain*. New York, NY: McKay.

Cassel, C.A. & Lo, C.C. (1997). Theories of Political Literacy. *Political Behavior*, 19 (4), 317–335.

Commission (2001). *Eurobarometer 5; Les Jeunes Europeens en 2001*. Luxembourg: Office for Official Publications of the European Communities. http://ec.europa.eu/public_opinion/archives/ebs/ebs_151_fr.pdf. (Summary in English: Young Europeans in 2001; Results of a European opinion poll. (http://ec.europa.eu/public_opinion/archives/ebs/ebs_151_summ_en.pdf)

Commission (2005). *Flash Eurobarometer 172*. Luxembourg: Office for Official Publications of the European Communities.

Commission (2008). *Eurobarometer 70; Public Opinion in the European Union*. Luxembourg: Office for Official Publications of the European Communities.

Commission (2009). *Eurobarometer 70; Public Opinion in the European Union, National Report The Netherlands*. Luxembourg: Office for Official Publications of the European Communities.

Converse, Ph. E. (1975). Public opinion and voting behavior. In N. Polsby & F. Greenstein (Eds.), *Handbook of political science* (p. 100–107). Volume 4. Reading, MA: Addison-Wesley.

Dekker, H. (1988). Europe in the classroom; European socialization and education. In P. Hübner (Ed.), *Lehrerbildung in Europa von den Herausforderungen der 90er Jahre* (p. 347–358). Berlin: Freie Universität.

Dekker, H. (1991). Political socialization in Europe. In H. Dekker & R. Meyenberg (Eds.), *Politics and the European younger generation; Political socialization in Eastern, Central and Western Europe* (p. 31–50). Oldenburg, FRG: BIS.

Dekker, H. (1992). Perceptions of the European Community. In R. Meyenberg & H. Dekker (Eds.), *Perceptions of Europe in East and West* (p. 41–64). Oldenburg: BIS.

Dekker, H. (1994). Political Competence of the Younger Generation in Western Europe: Creating a Context for Future National and European Political Socialization Research. In R. Farnen (Ed.), *Nationalism, Ethnicity, and Identity: Cross National and Comparative Perspective* (p. 427–439). New Brunswick, NJ: Transaction.

Dekker, H. & Nuus, M. (2007). Political knowledge and its origins, including cognitive ability, political motivations, political cynicism, political education, and political and civic participation. In P. Massing (Ed.), *Wirkungsforschung zur politischen Bildung im europäischen Vergleich* (p. 27−44). Schwalbach/Ts: Wochenschau Verlag.

Dekker, H. & Portengen, R. (2000). Political Knowledge: Theories and Empirical Research. In R.F. Farnen, H. Dekker, D.B. German & R. Meyenberg (Eds.), *Democracies in Transition. Political culture and Socialization Transformed in West and East* (p. 44−74).Oldenburg: BIS.

Delli Carpini, M. & Keeter, S. (1991). Stability and change in the U.S. public's knowledge of politics, *Public Opinion Quaterly*, 55, 583−612.

Delli Carpini, M. & Keeter, S. (1993). Measuring political knowledge: putting first things first, *American Journal of Political Science*, 37, 4, 117−206.

Delli Carpini, M. & Keeter, S. (1996). *What Americans Know about Politics and Why it Matters*. New Haven, NY: Yale University Press.

Dow, J. K. (2009). Gender Differences in Political Knowledge: Distinguishing Characteristics-based and Return-based Differences. *Political Behavior* 31, 117-136.

Farnen, R. F., Dekker, H., German, D. B. & Meyenberg, R. (Eds.) (2000). *Democracies in Transition; Political Culture and Socialization Transformed in West and East.* Oldenburg: BIS.

Farnen, R.F., Dekker, H., De Landtsheer, Chr., Sünker, H. & German, D.B. (Eds.) (2005). *Democratization, Europeanization, and Globalization Trends*. Frankfurt am Main: Peter Lang.

Galston, W.A. (2001). Political Knowledge, Political Engagement and Civic Education. *Annual Review Political Science*, 4, 217−234.

Hahn, C.L. (1998). *Becoming Political. Comparative Perspectives on Citizenship Education.* New York: State University of New York.

Lister, I. (1976). *Aims and methods of political education in schools.* Paper for the Conference on the development of democratic institutions in Europe. Strasbourg: Council of Europe.

Luskin, R.C. (1987). Measuring Political Sophistication. *American Journal of Political Science*, 31, 856−899.

Luskin, R.C. (1990). Explaining Political Sophistication. *Political Behavior* 12, 331−361.

Luskin, R.C. (2002). From denial to extenuation (and finally beyond): political sophistication and citizen performance. In Kuklinski, J.H. (Ed.), *Thinking about political psychology*. Cambridge, UK: Cambridge University Press.

Marcus, G.E. (2003). The Psychology of Emotion and Politics. In D.O. Sears, L. Huddy & R. Jervis (Eds.), *Oxford Handbook of Political Psychology* (p. 182−221). Oxford: Oxford University Press.

Milner, H. (2002). *Civic Literacy. How Informed Citizens Make Democracy Work.* Hanover, NH: University Press of New England.

Mondak, J.J. (2001). Developing valid knowledge scales, *American Journal of Political Science*, 45 (1), 224–238.

Muxel, A. (2001). *L'expérience politique des jeunes.* Paris: Presses des Sciences Po.

O'Toole, Th., Marsh, D. & Jones, S. (2003). Political literacy cuts both ways: The politics of non-participation among young people. *The Political Quarterly*, 74 (3), 349–360.

Popkin S.L. & Dimock, M.A. (1999). Political knowledge and citizen competence. In S.K. Elkin & K.E. Soltan (Eds.), *Citizen Competence and Democratic Institutions* (p. 117–146). University Park: Penn. State University Press.

Popkin, S.L. & Dimock, M.A. (2000). Knowledge, Trust, and International Reasoning. In A. Lupia, M. McCubbins & S.L. Popkin (Eds.), *Elements of Reason: Cognition, Choice, and the Bounds of Rationality* (p. 214–238). New York: Cambridge University Press.

Sears, D.O. (2003). Childhood and Adult Political Development. In D.O. Sears, L. Huddy & R. Jervis (Eds.), *Oxford Handbook of Political Psychology* (p. 60–109). Oxford: Oxford University Press.

Torney-Purta, J., Lehmann, R., Oswald, H. & Schulz, W. (2001). *Citizenship and Education in Twenty-eight Countries. Civic Knowledge and Engagement at Age Fourteen.* Amsterdam: The International Association for the Evaluation of Educational Achievement.

The test of WebQuest in Tallinn

Marti Taru

1. Introduction

The aim of this chapter is to assess the use of the WebQuest and conventional teaching method in terms of the difference in study results. The empirical analysis focuses on the analysis of test results, as the students' knowledge level and consequently their study results are characterised by the results of the tests carried out before and after the series of lessons. The central research question of this chapter is as follows: is there any difference between the test results of the students who attended lessons where WebQuest was used and of those who attended lessons where conventional teaching methods were used? The question consists of two sub-questions. Firstly, is there any difference in the extent of knowledge? Secondly, is there any difference in the extent of knowledge change? In other words, are there any systematic differences in the test results of the WebQuest and control groups?

The chapter begins with an overview of the curricula in Estonia, the course and time schedule of the project, data, the methods of data analysis and the results of the analysis.

2. Overview of Estonian schooling system

In Estonia, basic education can be acquired in primary schools (grades 1-6), basic schools (grades 1-9) or upper secondary schools that have opened basic school grades. Basic school is divided into three stages of study:

stage I: grades 1-3;
stage II: grades 4-6;
stage III: grades 7-9.

Basic education can be acquired on the basis of three national curricula: the national basic school and upper secondary school curriculum, the simplified national basic school curriculum and the national curriculum for students with moderate and severe learning disabilities (Estonian Ministry). The schools that participated in the project offered lessons on the basis of regular national curriculum. There are 15 compulsory subjects in basic schools. The national curriculum includes three subjects which more or less directly contribute to understanding society and social processes: Anatomy and Human Education, History and Social

Education. The curriculum of a school should include the following number of lessons per week per subject (Basic Schools):

Table 1
School stages and classes in Estonia

	Stage 1, Grades 1-3	Stage 2, Grades 4-6	Stage 3, Grades 7-9
History	0	3	6
Anatomy and human education	3	2	1
Social education	0	1	2

The schools that participated in the project taught the three subjects contributing to the understanding of society according to the number of lessons set in the curriculum. Although the number of music lessons and English lessons was bigger in some classes, the scope of social education subjects remained the same.

In the classes participating in this study, the subjects directly related to the understanding of society were taught in the same manner as in other schools. It means that it is possible to extend the results concerning social education to other schools and students who study according to the national curriculum.

4. Study session and testing in schools

The study session in the schools comprised four lessons that introduced the topics in the Teacher's Handbook. Whereas in the group that used WebQuest, the teacher basically had to support and help students in using WebQuest or give them practical feedback, the tasks of the teacher were more versatile in the groups that used conventional teaching and included preparing lessons, delivering them and giving feedback, if necessary. The teachers of this group were more independent in planning the content and the form of lessons, provided that the topics given in the Teacher's Handbook were covered.

Before preparing the lessons, there were meetings held with the school management and teachers. The aim of the meetings was to explain the purpose of the project and its methods both to the school management as well as to the teachers who would give the lessons. If necessary, meetings with teachers continued during the study session as well.

The lessons were delivered from October 2008 to January 2009. The time period depended on the school's and teachers' possibilities to schedule the four lessons in one row, and it does not mean that these four lessons were distributed over a long period of time. In most classes, tests were carried out by persons who were not from the same school.

5. Assessment model

Two models were used to assess the efficiency of the teaching method; the first was the bivariate model, which was followed by the multivariate model. The conceptual model containing two variables presents the research question on the graphic model below (Figure 1). According to this model, the share of correct answers and improvements in test results depend on the teaching method. Based on the understanding, which forms the basis of this research project, it could be reasonably assumed that different teaching methods will give different results in the extent of the change in the share of correct answers.

Figure 1. Bivariate model

Bivariate models typically present oversimplified picture of reality. In the case of our project it means that the correctness of answers depends also on other factors in addition to the teaching method. For instance, the correctness of answers can be associated with the replier's identity (students who identify themselves more strongly with Europe might know more about Europe and be more responsive to information); age (older students might know more, they also have more advanced conceptual networks that help them get new information more quickly); the number of books at home (students who have more books at home might be ready to learn more quickly and might have more profound knowledge of Europe).

A more detailed overview of theoretically expected co-variations between different variables and test responses is presented in the chapter by Eck and Weisseno. In addition to direct effects, the independent variables can be inter-correlated and thus the combinations of independent variables might have impact as well. For instance, attitudes towards the European Union can depend on the replier's home atmosphere and nationality or on the teaching method in a class. Further, one should not ignore the causal connections between independent variables themselves, e.g. the 'number of books at home' variable might influence attitudes towards the European Union and therefore the number of books at home is connected both directly and indirectly with the correctness of answers. In terms of empirical analysis, an analyst will have to sort direct effect from indirect and spurious effects, causal variables from preceding and intervening variables (Davis, 1985; Asher, 1983).

Still, the aim of this chapter is neither to develop a model that would specify the magnitude of each independent variable. The purpose of the empirical analysis is to minimise the impact of preceding and intermediating variables on the effect between the teaching method and test results and to bring out the direct effect between the two variables.

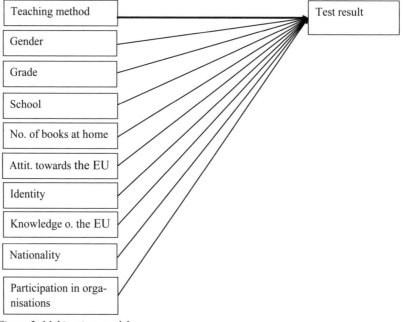

Figure 2. Multivariate model

6. Empirical analysis

Data collection was conducted in 2 schools in Tallinn. In both schools, 4 classes participated with class sizes around 30 pupils. Two of the classes did follow conventional lecturing classes on the topics and two did take the WebQuest classes.

Teaching was organised differently. In one of the schools, one teacher was responsible for delivering only conventional lessons and another teacher for delivering only WebQuest lessons. In another school, both teachers delivered both conventional and WebQuest lessons.

The table below (Table 2) shows the number of participating students from both schools. The number of students from both schools was more or less equal (the number of participants was in between 100 and 122). The number of students in the WebQuest group was between 50 and 58 and in the control group there were between 50 and 64 students.

Table 2
Number of pupils who participated either in pre- or post-lesson tests

	School No. 1		School No. 2	
	Pre-lessons	Post-lessons	Pre-lessons	Post-lessons
WebQuest group	54	56	58	50
Control group	54	53	64	50

The number of students who took both tests and whose test results could be matched before and after the lessons was somewhat smaller – only 157. The number of students in both groups decreased accordingly: the overall number of students from both schools in the WebQuest group was 77 and in the control group 80.

The student drop-out was caused by incidental absence during the tests and unclearly marked identification code that did not allow the two tests to be matched.

Table 3
Number of pupils who participated both in pre- and post-lesson tests

	School No. 1	School No. 2
WebQuest group	40	37
Control group	42	38

Description of pupils' social background is based on the data from post-lesson survey. Four characteristics of the sample will be reviewed in this section: Age, Class grade, Gender, Respondents' country of birth, Parents' country of birth, Language spoken at home.

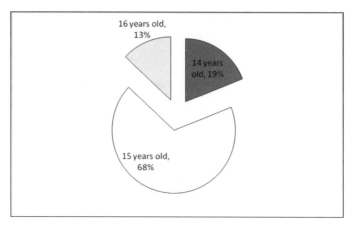

Figure 3. Age of paticipants

Two out of three pupils were 15 years old, one-fifth was 14 years old and approximately one-tenth was 16 years old. This age distribution represents class distribution of participants – out of 8 participating classes, 6 were grade 9 classes (75%).

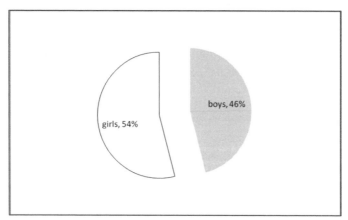

Figure 3. Gender of participants

The distribution by gender among the participants showed a fairly equal share of girls and boys.

The questionnaire gave the respondents an opportunity to mark all the languages they speak at home. The majority of the respondents marked only one language, although there were also respondents who spoke two languages (5% of the respondents) or even three languages (2%) at home. Judging by the first marked language, it can be clearly said that the participants formed a very homogenous group of students who speak Estonian at home:

Language at home Estonian – 99%
Language at home Russian – 1%

The answers of the students with several home languages were not analysed separately.

Nearly all respondents were of Estonian origin:

Respondent's country of birth Estonia – 97%
Respondent's mother's country of birth Estonia – 97%
Respondent's father's country of birth Estonia – 95%

Judging by the respondents' country of birth, their parents' country of birth and home language, it can be said that the sample is very homogenous. Homogeneity of the sample is even increased when language spoken at home is taken into account.

As a result, the results can be primarily extended to Estonians living in Estonia and should be extended to Russian-speaking population with caution. Differences in civic mindedness and attitudes between Estonians and non-Estonians are notable (Toots et al., 2006), which gives no justification to extending the results to non-Estonian category.

7. Data analysis methods

Bivariate analysis (presented graphically on Figure 1) focuses only on the correlation between the teaching methods and the correctness of answers. It is done by comparing the percentage of correct answers. This kind of analysis brings out an uncontroled co-variation between the variables, which might include also the impacts of different other variables (see Figure 2) on the test results and consequently also on the co-variation in question.

The multivariate model presented graphically on Figure 2 shows that test results depend, in addition to teaching method, also on a number of other factors. In this situation, the main goal of empirical analysis is to focus on direct effect between the two variables and to eliminate the impact of other variables. Regression analysis is the data analysis tool that meets those needs (Lewis-Beck, 1993). Amongst the variety of regression techniques, logistic regression was chosen. This method has been specially developed for the analysis of the dichotomous dependent variable model. It means that the dependent variable is not taken as an ordered sequence of values, but rather as the probability of the realisation of two values, which are related with the values of independent variables. This co-variation is not linear, but is expressed by a more advanced function – the logic function (Aldrich and Nelson, 1984). In this chapter we have two dichotomous dependent variables.

First, it is the variable that characterizes whether a pupil did give correct or incorrect answer to test question. Second, it is an index, which tells whether results of a pupil did improve between the two tests or did not improve.

As the objective of the current analysis is to find those independent variables which are to a significant extent correlated with the independent variable, the calculation of the actual values of the dependent variable – the identification of the probability of the realisation of one option – is not relevant. Our main purpose is to use the regression analysis to find independent variables that signficantly co-vary with the dependent variable. This information is provided by regression co-efficients.

The interpretation of the logistic regression coefficients is similar to the interpretation of the linear regression analysis. The positive value of the coefficient indicates the existence of a positive correlation (both the independent and dependent variable increase and decrease together) and the negative value shows that the correlation is negative (when one variable increases, the other decreases). To determine the statistical significance of a regression coefficient, the widely applied criterion of 5% significance level was used.

All questions in test sections 2 to 7 were used to evaluate the level of knowledge and the change in it, no selection was made amongst items.

First we examine percentage of correct answers and change in percentage of correct answers. For examining the effect of the 4-lesson teaching session, we compare percentages of pupils giving correct answers.

Differences between the WebQuest group and control group were gauged by comparing the differences of correct answers in both groups. The measure of difference between two distributions was the difference between percentages of correct answers. That measure was computed for each of the items in the test.

The Table 4 gives mean percentage of correct answers in WebQuest and conventional classes, for pre and post-lesson test scores as well as differences in scores.

Table 4
Mean percentage of correct answers and percentage difference

	% of correct answers before lessons	% correct answer after lessons	Difference after – before
WebQuest group	65%	61%	-3%
Control group	57%	60%	3%

The main result to be reported from the table is that on the average, the group which went through WebQuest lessons did not show any improvement in test results. On the contrary, the performance of the group showed a change for the worse: on the average, the percentage of correct answers dropped from 65% to 61%. The control group, on the other hand, showed some improvement: the percentage of correct answers went from 57% to 60%. There were no significant differences between sections of the questionnaire. In all sections, test results in the conventional group improved more than in the WebQuest group.

One can notice a difference in the pre-lesson test score in the two groups. While in the WebQuest group, 65% of respondents checked the correct box, while only 57% of responses did so in the control group.

As a hypothesis, one might propose an explanation that the control group showed improvement because it started from a lower percentage of correct answers and it was easier to improve one's results when starting from a lower base level.

The main goal of this section is to identify those background variables that co-vary with the correctness of responses. Analysis is based on the multivariate model in Figure 2. Logistic regression was used for identifying the independent variables that had a significant direct effect on the dependent variables.

The summarised results of the analysis are presented in the table below. The 'independent variable' column gives a short description of the independent variable; 'Number' shows the indicators used to measure the knowledge of the European Union or the number of dependent variables, which had a regression coefficient different from zero; the 'Mean' column shows the average value of the regression coefficients that did not equal zero.

The following overall table presents a number of important results. Firstly, it is clearly seen that the teaching method did not have any actual correlation with giving correct or wrong answers to test questions. Only in two questions of the overall 53 did the correlation not equal zero and in case of these two, the correlations are running counter. Therefore, it is not reasonable to assume that a teaching method is connected with the results.

The variable that is most clearly connected with the variables characterising knowledge is the grade. Ninth-graders had a higher probability of giving correct answers than the eighth-graders. The same correlation was evident in all 23 variables that had a regression coefficient other than zero. The finding confirms earlier findings in Estonia and has been related to the effect of passing the subjects that explain functioning of society (Toots et al., 2006, p. 21).

The respondent's gender was another variable that was correlated with the probability of giving correct answers to many knowledge-related questions. In case of girls, the probability of correct answers was higher than in case of boys.

The third and fourth important variables were the number of books at home and self-estimation of one's knowledge of the European Union. The correlation was positive in both variables: more books at home and higher self-estimation of knowledge were correlated with the higher probability of correct answers.

Table 5
Co-variants of the level of knowledge

Independent variable	Number	Mean
Teaching method	2	0.0
School	6	0.0
Gender	15	1.0
Grade	23	1.2
Number of books at home	11	0.4
Participation in youth organisations	4	0.4
Participation in cultural organisations	4	0.6
Interest in politics	4	0.3
Interest in the EU	2	-0.2
Knowledge of the EU	11	0.6
Identification with the place of residence	3	-0.6
Identification with the country of residence	1	-0.5
Identification with the EU	1	-0.5
EU policies encourage me to feel positive.	5	-0.6
Big countries benefit most from the EU.	2	0.6
Poorer countries benefit most from the EU.	5	-0.6
A good EU citizen informs her/himself about each political party's attitude to the EU before s/he votes.	2	-0.1
A good EU citizen is able to present a case why s/he is for or against a particular EU policy.	6	-0.7

The correlations of the remaining independent variables with the variables showing the level of knowledge were weaker or practically nonexistent.

Based on the evident correlations, one can sketch a very general profile of the student who would probably give the right answers. She is a ninth-grader, from a home with a lot of books and estimates her knowledge of the European Union fairly highly. Unfortunately, this model does not include the teaching method, which might be one of the factors that might influence the level of knowledge of the European Union.

For estimating and analysing changes in test scores, a new variable was computed. It has two values: '0' and '1'. The variable takes value 1 if post-lesson response was correct AND pre-lesson response was incorrect. The variable takes value '0' in all other cases.

The value '1' is easily interpreted since it contains only one group of pupils – only those whose test result improved. However, category '0' covers very different students. It includes students who gave correct or wrong answers to both tests as well as those who gave correct answers to the first test and wrong answers to the second test. Their only common feature is the fact that none of them got better test results.

Similarly to the analysis of the correctness of test answers, the analysis of the change consists of two parts: first, the comparison of the percentage of positive change, and next the identification of these independent variables, which are correlated with the change.

The results of the first part of data analysis are shown in Table 6 below. The table presents the average percentage shares of students who got better test results in both groups.

Table 6
Average percentages of pupils, who improved their test result

WebQuest group	Control group
15%	16%

It can be seen that in comparison with the WebQuest group, the results in the control group have improved more by one percentage point. However, the difference is so small that it cannot be taken as a significant one. In the bivariate model the result is to be interpreted as indicating that there is no signficant covariation between the teaching method and improved test results.

We will proceed by analysing the correlation between improved test results and independent variables. The dependent variables in this case are the indices that indicate the improvement of test results, while the independent variables are the same background variables that already were used for analysing the probability of correct answers. The method of logistic regression analysis was used for data analysis. The presentation of the results coincides with the presentation of the re-sults of the previous analysis (Table 5) – the first column gives a short description of an independent variable, the second column gives the number of indices it was significantly correlated with and the third column gives mean of significant regres-sion coefficients.

In analysing the correlation between improved test results and background variables, one can notice that independent variables were only weakly related to the knowledge improvement indices.

Teaching method is one of the background variables, which is statistically significant in the case of five indices. On the average, the correlation is positive which is interpreted that the probability of better results in the WebQuest group is somewhat higher than in the control group.

Another variable statistically significantly connected with five indices is the number of books at home. But in this case the mean of regression coefficients is negative, meaning that fewer books at home and higher probability of improved results go together. The finding has no easy substantive interpretation since higher number of books as a proxy for higher level of cultural capital at home can be exptected to go hand in hand with increased probability of improving test results.

Table 7
Co-variants of the change in the level of knowledge

Independent variable	Number	Mean
Teaching method	5	0.6
School	2	-1.2
Gender	2	-1.4
Grade	1	-1.0
Number of books at home	5	-0.5
Participation in youth organisations	1	3.0
Participation in cultural organisations	2	1.4
Interest in politics	1	0.5
Interest in the EU	3	-0.8
Knowledge of the EU	4	0.0
Identification with the place of residence	1	1.0
Identification with the country of residence	2	0.9
Identification with the EU	1	-2.5
EU policies encourage me to feel positive.	5	0.8
Big countries benefit most from the EU.	3	-0.8
Poorer countries benefit most from the EU.	4	0.5
A good EU citizen informs her/himself about each political party's attitude to the EU before s/he votes.	4	-0.4
A good EU citizen is able to present a case why s/he is for or against a particular EU policy.	4	0.0

The third variable connected with five indices is the estimation of feelings created by the European Union. Taking into account the coding of answers, the mean of the regression coefficients indicates that disagreement to the statement 'the European Union encourages positive feelings in me' goes together with the higher probability of improved results. Again, there is no good interpretation to this finding. By increasing learning motivation, positive attitude toward the EU could be expected to increase also learning gain but this was not the case here.

In case of the two variables – evaluation of one's knowledge of the European Union and the understanding that 'a good citizen of the European Union is able to present a case why s/he is for or against a particular EU policy' – the mean of the regression coefficients equals zero. Interpretation of the finding would be that there is no systematic co-variation between improved test results and the respective variable. The result runs counter to an hypothetical explanation that those who value rationality and knowledge also learn more eagerly.

However, the belief that 'a good citizen is informed of the views of political parties' is also connected with four indices; the mean of coefficients is negative. It tells us that those who agree with the statement tended to correct their answers more than those who disagreed with the statement. This finding diverts from the previous finding that there is no substantive connection between valuing knowledge and rationality and improving one's test results.

The belief that 'poorer countries benefit most from the European Union' is statistically significantly connected with four indices as well; the mean of coefficients is positive. Technically speaking, those who do not agree with the understanding that poorer countries benefit most from the European Union tended to correct their answers more than those who agreed with the statement.

The analysis of regression coefficients does not reveal patterns of systematic and internally harmonious co-variations between variables. When taken separately, the results do not oppose sound reason, contradictions become visible when one attempts to integrate the findings into a whole. Therefore it is not possible to give a general profile of the student who's test results improved most as we did in the part that analysed the correctness of answers.

The controversies also pose a challenge to the interpretation of co-variations found between the teaching method and improved results. Although the probability of better results was somewhat higher in the WebQuest group, controversies associated with other coefficients do not allow to interpret it as indicating better results of the WebQuest method. The adequate interpretation of this finding requires further exploration of the topic, starting from the formulation of the research question and the development of the theoretical model. Also the method of data collection should be given its due attention.

Hypothetical explanations why lessons did not improve significantly pupils' knowledge consist of more than one factor. The topic of European Union, as it was presented in the Teacher Handbooks, was too complicated for 8th and 9th grade pupils (Taru, 2009). The theme of developing civic identity through the subject of civic education actually is a very complex matter (Michaels & Stevick, 2009) so that successful delivery of the content would require pupils' full attention. Actually, teachers needed to fit the lessons into their curriculum as additional lessons, which did increase both teachers' and pupils' workload and perhaps decreased motivation to work on the themes. The latter might have influenced test results even though 18-year-olds Estonians' results in international comparison have been amongst top countries (Amadeo et al., 2002, p. 57).

8. Conclusion

In Tallinn, the lessons and tests that were compiled to study the efficiency of the WebQuest teaching method were performed from October 2008 to February 2009. There were 230 students from two Estonia-speaking schools in Tallinn who participated in either pre- or post-lesson test and 157 students who took both pre- and post-lesson tests. The results of data analysis did not prove that the WebQuest teaching method was more efficient than conventional teaching. Test results indicated that the share of correct answers in the WebQuest group was not higher and the test results did not improve either. While the analysis of correct answers makes it possible to draw a profile of the student who probably gave correct answers – a girl from the ninth grade who estimates her knowledge of the European Union as good and comes from a family with a rich cultural background – the analysis of the improvement of test results does not enable such a general profile to be sketched.

References

Amadeo, J.A., Torney-Purta, J., Lehmann, R., Husfeldt, V. & Nikolova, R. (2002). *Civic Knowledge and Engagement. An IEA Study of Upper Secondary Students in Sixteen Countries.* Amsterdam: IEA Secretariat.

Aldrich, J.H. & Nelson, F.D. (1984). *Linear Probability, Logit, and Probit Models.* Sage University Paper series on Quantitative Applications in the Social Sciences, 07–045. Beverly Hills and London: Sage Pubns.

Asher, H.B. (1983). *Causal Modeling.* Sage University Paper series on Quantitative Applications in the Social Sciences, 07–003. Beverly Hills and London: Sage Pubns.

Basic Schools and Upper Secondary Schools Act. (enacted 1993).

Davis, J.A. (1985). *The Logic of Causal Order.* Sage University Paper series on Quantitative Applications in the Social Sciences, 07–055. Beverly Hills and London: Sage Pubns.

Estonian Ministry of Education and Research. http:// www.hm.ee/index.php?1510026

Lewis-Beck, M.S. (Ed.) (1993). *Regression Analysis.* International Handbooks of Quantitative Applications in the Social Sciences, Vol. 2. London: Thousand Oaks and New Dehli: Sage Publications.

Michaels, D.L. & Stevick E.D. (2009). Europeanization in the 'other' Europe: writing the nation into 'Europe' education in Slovakia and Estonia. *Journal of Curriculum Studies*, 41, 225–245.

Taru, M. (2009). *Teacher feedback on using WebQuest and on lessons in Estonia. Interim report. Project „Teacher Empowerment to Educate Students to Become Active European Citizens (TEESAEC)".* Unpublished manuscript.

Toots, A., Idnurm, T. & Ševeljova, M. (2006). *Noorte kodanikukultuur muutuvas ühiskonnas /Youth Civic Culture in a Changing Society/* Tallinn.

Learning about European issues and institutions – An intervention study in Austrian schools

Reinhold Gaertner & Bernhard Natter[1]

1. Methodical procedure and theoretical background

The progresses in learning, the increase in knowledge of the European Union were examined in accordance with a targeted didactic intervention in four schools in Austria in the spring of 2008.[2] The prior knowledge of students in the 9th school form was ascertained at first in a pre-test; following 4 teaching units (lessons) the increase in knowledge was checked in a post-test. Thereby and through the feedback of the teachers participating, conclusions could be drawn on the usability of the teaching materials.

The school classes worked with the teaching materials either in the form of a WebQuest or with the same texts in printed form. In the WebQuest, the independent information search is guided in a structured form via more or less open problems in an internet-based learning environment. The students solve independently individual work tasks with the help of online materials. The comparison of the results of the WebQuest classes with the others was intended to give information on the efficiency of the WebQuest method.

Didactically and methodically, the series of lessons was geared to a "Europe-centred didactics of political science" (Weisseno, 2004; see also Rappenglueck, 2005) and competence-orientated lessons (with regard to Competence Orientation in Civic Education, see GPJE, 2004, p. 13–18; Krammer, 2008).

The case study of the planned ordinance of the EU Commission on the reduction of CO_2 emissions with new cars shall make clearer to the students the development and interaction of the EU institutions in the interplay with pressure groups in society. The series of lessons takes their orientation from the didactical principles of exemplary learning (Grammes, 2005a), problem orientation (Breit, 2005) and controversy (Grammes, 2005b), and the three dimensions of the political field, the relation of political content (policy), political process (politics) and political institutions (polity) (see e.g. Meyer, 2006, p. 83ff.). A traditional knowledge of in-

1   We would like to take the opportunity to thank very much Silvia Haslhofer and Stefan Triendl for the data input and the initial evaluation of the data.

2   The study was carried out at three schools in Tirol (BG/BRG Reithmannstraße Innsbruck, BHAK/BHAS Schwaz, HTL II Bau und Kunst Innsbruck) and one in Vorarlberg (BHAK/BHAS Lustenau). We would like to express our gratitude to the teachers Herbert Gasparin, Richard Hussl, Oswald Kollreider, Angelika Perkhofer and Manfred Hagen und their students for their engagement in the study.

stitutions is just not intended here. The case study shows the institutions with their varied positions of interests and these in action, in the negotiating processes with societal players (lobbyism) in the European multilayered system.

The teaching materials developed by the TEESAEC project group shall foster the development of key concepts on the EU. Such concepts contribute via the ability of abstraction to developing a conceptual knowledge which makes an input to political orientation, if it is transferable, if thereby other daily political events and processes at the European level can be better analytically considered and classified. (With regard to conceptual knowledge, see the article of Weisseno & Eck: Concepts on the European Union in the present volume; Kuehberger, 2009)

The category of conceptual knowledge had large effects on the designing of the questionnaire for the pre- and post-test. In order to obtain indications on the possible transfer of concepts learned in the lessons to other examples of European politics, simple concrete knowledge of facts was not asked about in the post-test. Rather more, the questionnaire contains other concrete examples on European politics, but underlying which are to be found similar key concepts like in the teaching materials. The question of a possible increase in knowledge is directed more at the level of abstract concepts than at simple facts.

The differences between the pre-test and the post-test are especially analysed at two levels:

at the level of different concepts in terms of content as building blocks for developing conceptual knowledge;

at the level of different methodical approches: WebQuest classes versus classes with printed materials.

In addition, relations are also examined between students with or without migration backgrounds and with different educational backgrounds in the categories of political interests, political activities and political attitudes.

2. Results in the post-test

On the whole, it can be stated that the results of the post-test were mostly better (but not in all categories) than those of the pre-test. In detail, this appears as follows:

National Interest

4 students were not able to answer any single question correctly in the post-test. In total, the results of both the tests were relatively similar: 5 or 6 correct answers were given in the pre-test by 53.6%, in the post-test by 52.2% of the respondents.

A very high percentage rate could give the right answer two-times (between 67% and 84%); the improvements lay between 30% and 54%.

Table 1
National Interest

Questions	Improvement pre-/ post-test in %	In both cases correct answer in %
25	54	84
26	52	77
39	38	67
43	40	80
47	37	67
48	30	76

Pressure Groups

There was a clear increase in the Pressure Groups category with six correct answers: if only two were able to answer all the questions correctly in the pre-test, there were 10 in the post-test. Five or six right answers were given by 33.3% in the pre-test, in the post-test by 32% of the respondents. In the post-test, a relatively large percentage rate of the students was able to respectively improve:

Question 14: 43%; question 27: 64%; question 28: 48%; question 32: 40% and question 33: 53%. In both cases, the correct answer was given by between 53% and 85% of the respondents.

Table 2
Pressure Groups

Questions	Improvement pre-/ post-test in %	In both cases correct answer in %
14	43	80
27	64	85
28	48	73
29	50	59
32	40	53
33	53	70

European Parliament

In this category, there were hardly any changes: one resp. three students were not able to answer any question correctly, in each case just under 16% (15.6%, resp. 15.9%) gave six or seven correct answers.

The percentage rate of those students who gave the correct answer two times (between 59% and 70%) was somewhat lower here than with categories 1 and 2. An exception was question 60 with 80%. The improvements lay between 21% and 44% – again with the exception of question 60 (60%).

Table 3
European Parliament

Questions	Improvement pre-/ post-test in %	In both cases correct answer in %
16	36	70
17	44	68
57	27	73
58	21	32
59	36	62
60	60	83
61	36	59

European Commission

There is again a clear increase to be ascertained. If at first 20% of the respondents were able to give six or seven correct answers, then this percentage rate lay at 27.5% in the post-test. Only two persons in the pre-test but 8 in the post-test could answer all seven questions correctly.

The improvements Pre-/Post-test were somewhat lower marked than with "Pressure Groups", nevertheless, a relatively high percentage rate was able to give the correct answer both times in the case of almost all the questions (with the exception of question 63).

Table 4
European Commission

Questions	Improvement pre-/ post-test in %	In both cases correct answer in %
18	53	70
30	56	69
36	37	75
37	63	76
44	35	75
62	34	63
63	37	30

Cooperation of the Institutions

Also in this category, there were very clear increases. 22.6% answered five or six answers correctly in the pre-test, this percentage rate rose to 37.3% in the post-test. The rise was particularly striking in that group which answered all six questions correctly: at first 6%, in the post-test 16.4%. Five persons in contrast to solely two in the pre-test were, however, not able to answer any of the questions correctly. In a large part of the cases, there were only small improvements between both tests.

The values for those who answered both times correctly were spread well apart (between 23% and 83%).

Table 5
Cooperation of the Institutions

Questions	Improvement pre-/ post-test in %	In both cases correct answer in %
19	26	31
20	21	23
21	56	59
22	41	77
31	29	82
51	13	27
64	38	53
65	39	61

European Interest
In contrast, there was a slight reversal in the data with this category: 69.5% had four or even five correct answers in the pre-test, 62.3% in the post-test. The values for all five correct answers were with 44% (post-test), resp. 37.7% relatively high.

With 73%–83%, there were absolutely high values for those who gave the correct answer twice. Relatively low was the improvement with question 24, relatively high with the other three questions (60%–69%).

Table 6
European Interest

Questions	Improvement pre-/ post-test in %	In both cases correct answer in %
23	63	83
24	23	80
38	69	79
45	60	73

Global Issues/Rights
47.8% were able to give five or six correct answers in the pre-test, in the post-test even 58.4%. The proportion of those who gave fewer than three correct answers dropped from 20.2% (pre-test) to 12.3%.

In both cases, correct answers were given by between 67% and 87%; improvements ranged from 33% (question 49) to 83% (question 83).

Table 7
Global Issues/Rights

Questions	Improvement pre-/ post-test in %	In both cases correct answer in %
46	42	67
49	33	64
50	43	80
52	83	87
53	67	82
55	19	79

Council of Ministers
In the eighth category, there were hardly any measurable increases. 3%, resp. 4.5% knew how to answer all the questions correctly, 15.2%, resp. 14.9% had six right answers and one wrong answer.

In the case of questions on the Council of Ministers category, the values for answering correctly two times were between 55% and 78%; improvements between 13% (question 40) and 56% (question 34).

Table 8
Council of Ministers

Questions	Improvement pre-/ post-test in %	In both cases correct answer in %
15	55	78
34	56	61
35	42	73
40	13	25
41	31	48
42	26	65
54	32	74
56	32	55

3. Comparison of WebQuest versus control classes according to concepts

National Interest
The WebQuest classes could maintain the high level of the pre-test (67.5% five or six correct answers) in the post-test with 64.1%. The control classes had the respective results of 34.5% (pre-test), resp. 36.6% (post-test).

No increase could be ascertained in the categorization very good – good – poor undertaken with the WebQuest groups; with the control groups, a slight deterioration.

Table 9
National interest

			Block of questions: National interest		Block of questions: National interest PoT	
			Number	Number of scales (%)	Number	Number of scales (%)
Group category	WebQuest	poor	0	0	1	2.6
		good	13	32.5	13	33.3
		very good	27	67.5	25	64.1
	Control class	poor	2	6.9	7	23.3
		good	17	58.6	12	40.0
		very good	10	34.5	11	36.7

Table 10
Pressure groups

			Block of questions: Pressure groups		Block of questions: Pressure groups PoT	
			Number	Number of scales (%)	Number	Number of scales (%)
Group category	WebQuest	poor	1	2.5	1	2.5
		good	24	60.0	23	57.5
		very good	15	37.5	16	40.0
	Control class	poor	0	0	4	13.3
		good	21	72.4	21	70.0
		very good	8	27.6	5	16.7

Striking in this category was the increase in those students who were able to answer all the questions correctly. No-one in the WebQuest group was able to do so in the pre-test, in the post-test there were nine. 37.5% (pre-test), resp. 40% in the post-test could answer five or six questions correctly; in the control group, there were 27.6%, resp. 16.6%.

The categorization very good – good – poor shows in the case of the WebQuest groups a stagnation (at a very high level); there was a slight deterioration with the control groups.

Table 11
European Parliament

			Block of questions: European Parliament		Block of questions: European Parliament PoT	
			Number	Number of scales (%)	Number	Number of scales (%)
Group category	WebQuest	poor	1	2.9	1	2.6
		good	16	45.7	20	51.3
		very good	18	51.4	18	46.2
	Control class	poor	3	10.3	7	23.3
		good	17	58.6	13	43.3
		very good	9	31.0	10	33.3

Table 12
European Commission

			Block of questions: European Commission		Block of questions: European Commission PoT	
			Number	Number of scales (%)	Number	Number of scales (%)
Group category	WebQuest	poor	0	0	2	5.1
		good	14	38.9	11	28.2
		very good	22	61.1	26	66.7
	Control class	poor	2	6.9	9	30.0
		good	17	58.6	12	40.0
		very good	10	34.5	9	30.0

European Parliament

There were hardly any changes in the WebQuest groups before and after the corresponding teaching units: 25.7% had six or seven correct answers in the pre-test in comparison to 25.6% in the post-test. No-one in the control groups could answer all seven questions correctly either in the pre-test or in the post-test, six correct answers were given in each case by one person. The WebQuest groups improve in the categorization very good – good – poor, the control groups fare somewhat worse in the category poor and in the category very good they show a slight improvement.

European Commission
The WebQuest group could increase from 27.8% to 35.9% in the area of six, resp. seven correct answers, the control group from 10.3% to 16.7% (table 12). Once again, there was no-one in the control group who had seven correct answers either in the pre-test or in the post-test. 2 of the WebQuest group could answer all the questions correctly in the pre-test, but 8 could do so in the post-test.

The WebQuest groups improve here (very good from 61.6% to 66.7%); the control groups worsen (very good from 34.5% to 30%; good from 58.6% to 40%).

Cooperation of the Institutions
On the whole, a clear increase can be ascertained in the category very good (from 27% to 45.9%); however, there is also an increase from 2.7% to 13.5% in the category poor. In the control group, the proportion of very good rises from 17.2% to 21.4%.

Table 13
Cooperation of the Institutions

			Block of questions: Co-operation of Institutions		Block of questions: Cooperation of Institutions PoT	
			Number	Number of scales (%)	Number	Number of scales (%)
Group category	WebQuest	poor	1	2.7	5	13.5
		good	26	70.3	15	40.5
		very good	10	27.0	17	45.9
	Control class	poor	3	10.3	7	25.0
		good	21	72.4	15	53.6
		very good	5	17.2	6	21.4

European Interest
Just under half of the respondents of the WebQuest group could answer all 5 questions correctly in the pre-test (47.5%; four or five 72.5%); in the post-test, 53.8% had five, 71.7% four or five correct answers. In comparison to this, the results in the pre-test were 34.5% with all five questions correct, 65.5% with four or five correct answers. In the post-test, however, there was a clear deterioration in this group (16.7% five, 50% four or five correct answers).

Interesting here is the rise with the category very good: WebQuest group from 0 to 53.6%, control group from 0 to 16.7%.

Table 14
European Interest

			Block of questions: European interest		Block of questions: European interest PoT	
			Number	Number of scales (%)	Number	Number of scales (%)
Group category	WebQuest	poor	3	7.5	2	5.1
		good	37	92.5	16	41.0
		very good	0	0	21	53.8
		poor	1	3.4	3	10.0
	Control Class	good	28	96.6	22	73.3
		very good	0	0	5	16.7

Global Issues/Rights

Pre-test and post-test results of the WebQuest groups were practically the same with 59.4%, resp. 59% (five or six correct answers); in the control group, there was a clear deterioration from 57.2% to 33.4%.

There were no improvements with the very good category of the WebQuest group (59.5% to 59%), but a deterioration in the control groups (57.1% to 33.3%).

Council of Ministers

In this category, there were likewise only slight changes with the WebQuest group (pre-test 27%, six or seven correct answers; post-test 23.2%); in the control group a rise from 6.9% to 14,2%.

There was an improvement in the categorization very good – good – poor with the WebQuest group; the control group showed a slight deterioration.

In general, the following results can be ascertained: It can be upheld that no deterioration was seen in general with the WebQuest classes, there were essentially either improvements or stagnation. It is also evident that the WebQuest classes absolutely fared better than the control classes. The latter once again could exhibit improvements in only a few cases. The best results for both groups were seen – both in the pre-test and post-test – in the categories European Interest, National Interest and Global Issues/Rights.

Table 15
Global issues/rights

			Block of questions: Global issues/rights		Block of questions: Global issues/rights PoT	
			Number	Number of scales (%)	Number	Number of scales (%)
Group category	WebQuest	poor	2	5.4	2	5.1
		good	13	35.1	14	35.9
		very good	22	59.5	23	59.0
	Control class	poor	1	3.6	3	10.0
		good	11	39.3	17	56.7
		very good	16	57.1	10	33.3

Table 16
Council of Ministers

			Block of questions: Council of Ministers		Block of questions: Council of Ministers PoT	
			Number	Number of scales (%)	Number	Number of scales (%)
Group category	WebQuest	poor	4	10.8	1	2.6
		good	16	43.2	19	48.7
		very good	17	45.9	19	48.7
	Control class	poor	0	0	5	17.9
		good	19	65.5	16	57.1
		very good	10	34.5	7	25.0

In the categories Pressure Groups, European Commission and Cooperation of the Institutions, there was on the whole a clearly positive increase; this was due primarily to improvements with the WebQuest group.

Stagnation (in both groups) was seen in the categories European Parliament and Council of Ministers.

Attitudes towards Politics
We have attempted to make a closer examination of the test results also in respect of the migration and educational background.

The following results can be stated: A relation between migration background and political interest is only very weakly marked; but anyhow students with a migration background showed slightly more interest in politics than those without this family background. However, it is to be taken into consideration that a high interest

Table 17
Migration background: Interest in politics

			Interest in politics			
			low	middle	high	Total
Migration back-ground	no	Number, % of migra-tion background	51 44.3	56 48.7	8 7.0	115 100.0
	yes	Number, % of migra-tion background	22 41.5	27 50.9	4 7.5	53 100.0
Total		Number, % of migra-tion background	73 43.5	83 49.4	12 7.1	188 100.0

Table 18.
Migration background: Activities in associations and other organizations

			Activity in clubs/associations			
			inactive	active	very active	Total
Migration back-ground	no	Number, % of migration background	45 39.8	55 48.7	13 11.5	113 100.0
	yes	Number, % of migration background	20 39.2	27 52.9	4 7.8	51 100.0
Total		Number, % of migration background		82 50.5	17 10.4	164 100.0

in politics with only 7% is generally a very weakly marked feature. There was prac-tically no difference ascertained with the question on actvity in associations or or-ganizations – both groups had 60% active, resp. very active, just under 40% inac-tive.

A result that was expected – because it was ascertained in a large number of other studies – was the answer to relations between migration background and edu-cation. Students with a migration background were clearly at a disadvantage. 67.9% of them had a low-level educational background (in comparison to 39.1% without a migration background), only 3.8% of the students with a migration back-ground but 18.3% of those without a migration background had a higher-level edu-cation background.

No significant difference exists with the answer to the question about migration background and self-estimation, resp. knowledge of the EU. Only about 10% of the students considered themselves to be well-informed on the EU.

Table 19
Migration background: Educational background

| | | | Educational background | | | Total |
			low	middle	high	
Migration back-ground	no	Number % of migra-tion background	45	49	21	115
			39.1	42.6	18.3	100.0
	yes	Number % of migrati-on background	36	15	2	53
			67.9	28.3	3.8	100.0
Total		Number % of migrati-on background	81	64	23	168
			48.2	38.1	13.7	100.0

Table 20
Migration background: Knowledge of the EU – self-estimation

| | | | Knowledge on the EU – self estimation | | | Total |
			low	middle	high	
Migration back-ground	no	Number, % of migra-tion background	60	43	12	115
			52.2	37.4	10.4	100.0
	yes	Number, % of migrati-on background	24	23	6	53
			45.3	43.4	11.3	100.0
Total		Number, % of migrati-on background	84	66	18	168
			50.5	39.3	10.7	100.0

There was a diffferent development in regard to the identification with the EU. 7.9% of those without and 3.8% of those with a migration background had a strong identification with the EU; thus it was to be seen in the aggregate score that 43% of the students with a migration background had an identification with the EU but only 30% of those without a migration background had this.

Even though there is on the whole no very significant relation between educational background and interest in politics, it can nevertheless be stated that 51% of the students with a low-level educational background but only 21.7% of those with a high-level one show little interest in politics; vice-versa were 5%, resp. 13% very interested in politics.

In a noteworthy manner, students with a high-level educational background record the lowest values with "very associated"; also with the aggregate score (27.2%), they lie well behind those with a low-level one (29.7%) but still very clearly trail behind those with an average-level educational background (43.7%). Those who were neutral in all three categories were between just under 40% and 50%.

There is a striking relation between interest in politics and activity in associations, resp. organizations. Solely 16.7% of those highly interested in politics were inactive, 58.3% were active and 25% were very active. The opposite was to be seen in the other categories: 13.6% of those interested in politics on an average level were very active, 53.1% active and 33.3% inactive, whereas those with little interest in politics were to 50.7% inactive, to 45.1% active and only to 4.2% very active.

Table 21
Migration background: Identification with the EU

			Identification with the EU					
			not at all associated	1	2	3	v. associated	Total
Migration background	no	Number	9	17	53	26	9	114
		% of migration background	7,9	14.9	46.5	22.8	7.9	100.0
	yes	Number	3	6	21	21	2	53
		% of migration background	5.7	11.3	39.6	39.6	3.8	100.0
Total		Number		23	74	47	11	167
		% of migration background		13.8	44.3	28.1	6.6	100.0

	not associated with EU	Neutral	associated with EU	Total
No migration background	26	53	35	114
	22.8	46.5	30.7	100
Migration background	9	21	23	53
	17.0	39.6	43.4	100

In summarizing, it can be stated that the school classes that worked with the Web-Quest method attained better results with the transfer of concepts of knowledge to other contexts. However, no statement can be made on the influence of various concrete teaching situations on this result. It was not ascertained how the teachers instructed their students and in which concrete learning situation the teaching took place.

Table 22
Educational background: Interest in politics

		Interest in politics			Total
		low	middle	high	
Educational	Low number	42	34	5	81
background	% of educational background	51.9	42	6.2	100
	Middle number	26	34	4	64
	% of educational background	40.6	53.1	6.3	100
	High number	5	15	3	23
	% of educational background	21.7	65.2	13.0	100
Total	Number	73	83	12	168
	% of educational background	43.5	49.4	7.1	100

Table 23
Educational background: Identification with the EU

		Interest in politics					Total
		not at all asso-ciated	1	2	3	very asso-ciated	
Educational	Low number	9	10	38	19	5	81
background	% of educational background	11.1	12.3	46.9	23.5	6.2	100
	Middle number	3	8	25	23	5	64
	% of educational background	4.7	12.5	39.1	35.9	7.8	100
	High number	0	5	11	5	1	22
	% of educational background	0	22.7	50.0	22.7	4.5	100
Total	Number	12	23	74	47	11	167
	% of educational background	7.2	13.8	44.3	28.1	6.6	100

Edu. background	not associated with EU	Neutral	associated with EU
Low	23.4	46.9	29.7
Middle	17.2	39.1	43.7
High	22.7	50.0	27.2

Table 24
Interest in politics: Activities in associations

| | | Activity in clubs/associations | | | |
		inactive	active	very active	Total
Educational background	Low number	36	32	3	71
	% of educational background	50.7	45.1	4.2	100
	Middle number	27	43	11	81
	% of educational background	33.3	53.1	13.6	100
	High Number	2	7	3	12
	% of educational background	16.7	58.3	25.0	100.0
Total	Number	65	82	17	164
	% of educational background	39.6	50.5	10.4	100

The feedback of the teachers that was obtained from all those participating in the project was on the whole positive. The method of the WebQuest was generally experienced as motivational for the students. The teaching materials and the choice of the case study were basically assessed as relevant and well-adaptable for a discourse with EU politics at school. In detail, the teachers criticized especially that some texts were too difficult to understand and the prescribed apportioning of the materials to four school lessons was estimated as too short in time. In respect of adapting the TEESAEC WebQuest for a general educational public, such critical points were taken into account (e.g. the material was newly apportioned to six teaching units).

References

Breit, G. (2005). Problemorientierung. In W. Sander (Ed.), *Handbuch politische Bildung* (p. 108−125). Bonn: Bundeszentrale für politische Bildung.

GPJE (Gesellschaft für Politikdidaktik und politische Jugend- und Erwachsenenbildung) (2004). *Nationale Bildungsstandards für den Fachunterricht in der Politischen Bildung an Schulen. Ein Entwurf.* Schwalbach/Ts.: Wochenschau Verlag.

Grammes, T. (2005a). Exemplarisches Lernen. In W. Sander (Ed.), *Handbuch politische Bildung* (p. 93−107) . Bonn: Bundeszentrale für politische Bildung.

Grammes, T. (2005b). Kontroversität. In W. Sander (Ed.), *Handbuch politische Bildung* (p. 126−145). Bonn: Bundeszentrale für politische Bildung.

Krammer, R. (2008). Kompetenzen durch Politische Bildung. Ein Kompetenz-Strukturmodell. In *Informationen zur Politischen Bildung,* 29, 5–14.

Kuehberger, Ch. (2009). Welches Wissen benötigt die politische Bildung? In: *Informationen zur Politischen Bildung,* 30, 52–56.

Meyer, T. (2006). *Was ist Politik?* Wiesbaden: VS Verlag für Sozialwissenschaften.

Rappenglueck, S. (2005). Europabezogenes Lernen. In W. Sander (Ed.), *Handbuch politische Bildung* (p. 456–468). Bonn: Bundeszentrale für politische Bildung.

Weisseno, G. (2004). Konturen einer europazentrierten Politikdidaktik. Europäische Zusammenhänge verstehen lernen. In G. Weisseno (Ed.), *Europa verstehen lernen. Eine Aufgabe des Politikunterrichts* (p. 108–125). Bonn: Bundeszentrale für politische Bildung.

Teachers' perceptions of student needs and identities: addressing local, national, European and international dimensions of citizenship and belonging

Audrey Osler & Nicola Savvides

1. Introduction

In this chapter, we discuss how teachers in three contrasting English schools understand their students' needs, as learners and as young citizens, and how these understandings impact on curriculum design and development, relating to local, national, European and international dimensions of citizenship.

The TEESAEC project had two main elements: curriculum materials design and research. The first element centred on the development of web-based materials (WebQuest), designed to be used in a range of European countries to support students as active European citizens. The international project team aimed to make a comparative analysis of students' knowledge of Europe and the European Union and to assess the impact of the web-based materials on students within selected schools in each nation-state.

No curriculum innovation (or research project) takes place in a vacuum; it is mediated by a range of political, cultural, institutional and other factors. We contend that the process of any curriculum implementation is likely to be influenced, in particular, by teachers' attitudes, professional skills, and their perceptions of the needs and identities of their students.

In this chapter we present qualitative research, designed to explore teachers' perceptions of the citizenship curriculum, set within a broader analysis of English education policy relating to citizenship, diversity and social cohesion. This dimension of the study provides a contextual setting for the implementation of the TEESAEC materials. We examine teachers' perceptions of their students' needs and identities as learner-citizens; how these perceptions influence pedagogical choices and preferences; and the relative importance teachers assign to local, national, European and global aspects of citizenship. Our aim is to explore how teachers interpret and mediate education policies and curriculum guidelines and how they make choices about curriculum design and pedagogy.

We begin by outlining recent policy developments in England, relating to the school curriculum and citizenship education. We discuss these within the context of political developments, which, we suggest, have influenced teachers' understandings of students' needs as learner-citizens with potential to engage at local, national, European and global scales. We discuss our findings, examining teachers' beliefs about their students in order to explore the relationship between these perceptions and teachers' choices about curriculum design and pedagogy.

2. Curriculum policy, citizenship education and diversity

Citizenship education is a relatively new element within the school curriculum in England. A national curriculum was first introduced under a Conservative government, following the Education Reform Act 1988. Before this, curriculum development and innovation generally took place at local levels, with schools and teachers exercising considerable autonomy. The original national curriculum was heavily criticised for its narrow focus and its failure to recognise Britain as a multicultural society (Tomlinson, 2009) and was characterized as a nationalistic curriculum which failed to prepare young people for life in an interdependent and globalized world.

Citizenship education was given consideration in the early 1990s within the framework of a national curriculum (Edwards & Fogelman, 1993) but it was in the late 1990s, following the election of a Labour government, that education for citizenship and democracy was placed centrally on the agenda. The publication of the Crick report (Qualifications and Curriculum Authority, 1998) sought to achieve cross-party consensus on the need for political education. The Crick report acknowledged long-standing cultural, political and religious diversity within British society and stressed the need for tolerance, but it presented democracy as a completed project, rather than as an on-going struggle, where race, gender and other inequalities persist (Osler, 2000). The overwhelming emphasis was on the nation-state, with a passing acknowledgment of Europe and European institutions, international human rights norms, and the wider global community.

Citizenship education was introduced in 2000 and became mandatory in secondary schools in 2002. The official report of the Stephen Lawrence Inquiry (Macpherson, 1999), led the government and the major opposition parties to acknowledge institutional racism as a feature of British society, committing themselves to address racism within public services, including the police force and education. The consequent Race Relations [Amendment] Act 2000 requires schools and other public bodies not only to address discrimination but also to promote race equality. Citizenship education was identified as the main vehicle through which this would be addressed within the curriculum. Political consensus on the need to tackle institutional racism was, however, short-lived. Some ten years later, there is evidence of widespread denial of the on-going impact of institutional racism on British society (Rollock, 2009).

Since the publication of the Crick report, there has been heightened debate in the UK about citizenship, multiculturalism and national identity. Following the 2005 London suicide bombings, senior government figures, including Prime Ministers Tony Blair and Gordon Brown, have both encouraged and provoked public debate about so-called 'British values' (Osler, 2009). Concerns about security and the prevention of extremism were added to the list of official justifications for the teaching of citizenship (Osler & Starkey, 2006); such concerns are codified in the Education and Inspections Act 2006 which requires schools to promote community cohesion. The Ajegbo report (Department for Education and Skills, 2007), proposed a new strand to the citizenship curriculum, entitled 'identity and diversity' and a closer link between history and citizenship learning, extending the framework of the Crick report but largely avoiding a critical examination or race and racism (Osler, 2008). Schools have thus been pinpointed as playing a key role in strengthening social cohesion, most notably through the promotion of British values that include duties to a common community (Brookes & Holford, 2009) through the teaching of citizenship and history.

Within publicly-funded secondary schools, history is mandatory at key stage three (for students aged 11-14 years) but optional beyond the age of 14, whereas citizenship is taught at key stages three and four, from age 11-16 years. Teachers are reminded that both subjects contribute to the broader aims of the national curriculum, a central goal of which is to enable young people to become 'responsible citizens who make a positive contribution to society' (QCA, 2007a, b & c). Citizenship is deemed important as it 'equips young people with the knowledge, skills and understanding to play an effective role in public life' and 'encourages them to take an interest in topical and controversial issues and to engage in discussion and debate' (QCA, 2007a, p. 27; QCA, 2007b, p. 44). Although this introductory statement mentions 'global citizens' and the differing scales in which young people can take an active role, namely, 'schools, neighbourhoods, communities and wider society' (QCA, 2007a, p. 27; QCA, 2007b., p. 44), the overriding emphasis is on the nation; the concept of European citizen is notable by its absence.

References to students' identities within the citizenship programme of study are largely related to learning to live together in a nation characterised by diversity. Commonality and social cohesion are stressed, as are the importance of respecting and learning about different 'ideas, beliefs, cultures and identities and the values we share as citizens in the UK' (QCA, 2007a, p. 27; 2007b, p. 41). The history curriculum also aims to encourage 'mutual understanding of the historic origins of our ethnic and cultural diversity' and the development of students' 'identities through an understanding of history at personal, local, national and international levels' (QCA, 2007c, p. 111). There is no explicit reference to students' identities as European citizens.

Britain's relationships and interconnections; the European Union; the wider Europe; the Commonwealth; the United Nations; and global community all feature (QCA, 2007a, p. 27, 33; QCA, 2007b, p. 41; QCA, 2007c, p. 111) but they take a second place to the role of citizens within a parliamentary democracy; the fundamentals of the justice system; and the concept of community cohesion.

At key stage four, there is slightly more emphasis on learning about international engagement, including 'actions citizens can take in democratic and electoral processes to influence decisions locally, nationally and beyond'; 'other forms of government, both democratic and non-democratic, beyond the UK'; and 'challenges facing the global community' such as international conflicts, inequality, and sustainability (QCA, 2007b, p. 46-47). Nevertheless, the focus remains primarily on what it means, politically and socially, to be a UK, rather than EU citizen.

The overriding emphasis is on *active* citizenship: for students to 'take action and try to make a difference in their communities and the wider world' (QCA, 2007a, p. 28; 2007b, p. 42). The starting point for such action is the school community and local communities.

3. Research method and context

We conducted semi-structured interviews with eight teachers in three secondary schools in the north of England which agreed to trial the TEESAEC web-based materials. A total of 239 students were involved in the TEESAEC project across these three schools. The teacher interviews were generally scheduled directly after the students had completed a set of four lessons focusing on the European Union. We interviewed both those teachers who had facilitated their students' use of the Web-Quest and those who had taught a series of four parallel lessons, addressing the same concepts and themes, but selecting their own pedagogical styles and materials.

The teachers all had responsibility for some aspect of citizenship learning, but had generally received little specific training. Some identified themselves as teachers of citizenship; whereas others saw themselves primarily as teachers of a related subject, such as history or geography. As well as seeking direct feedback on the materials, we invited the teachers to talk about their conceptions of citizenship; their understandings of European citizenship; and the priorities they give to different aspects of citizenship teaching and learning. Interviews were audio-recorded and transcribed for analysis.

The three research schools are all co-educational and non-selective in their student intake, but they differ in significant ways by social class, ethnic composition, and student achievement levels. Background data concerning the schools are drawn from the reports of the Office for Standards in Education (Ofsted), the school inspection agency for England.

Lambton School is situated in a market town serving students aged 11-18 from the town and surrounding villages. Although it draws students from a wide range of social backgrounds, the intake is largely white British, reflecting the composition of the local population. Middle class students are over-represented and the number of students eligible for free school meals (a proxy indicator of relative poverty) is very low. The school was recognised as a High Performing School by the Department of Education and Skills (DfES) in 2005 and the most recent inspection report, from 2006, states that the average attainment of school entrants is high and the proportion of students with learning difficulties below the national average. Citizenship is offered as a discrete timetabled subject, but citizenship issues are also addressed in other curriculum areas, most notably history. In addition, there is a range of opportunities for students to learn citizenship skills through extra-curricular activities.

Coalthorpe Community College serves students aged 11-18 and is situated in a former mining town with high levels of social deprivation and unemployment. This is reflected in the student population, which according to the latest inspection report, is working class, with an above average percentage entitled to free school meals. Students enter with below average attainment levels and the proportion of students with learning difficulties is higher than the national average. In 2006, Ofsted described the school as largely white British, with no students having English as an additional language. Since this time, Coalthorpe has admitted a number of migrant students from Poland and elsewhere in Eastern Europe. This factor attracted Coalthorpe teachers to the TEESAEC project; they hoped engagement in a European curriculum initiative would support the integration of newcomers into a relatively homogeneous school community. Citizenship at Coalthorpe Community College is largely taught through a new subject, 'Learning for Life'.

Hornby Road School serves students aged 11-18 in a large multicultural city and, according its 2008 inspection report, has a balanced mixture of students from middle class and working class families. There is a significant number of students from minority ethnic backgrounds (over twice the national average and growing) and also a high number of students for whom English is an additional language. The percentage of students entitled to free school meals is slightly above the national average, but the proportion with learning difficulties is below average. Citizenship education at Hornby Road is not timetabled as such; it is incorporated into other subjects using a cross-curricular model and through extra-curricular activities.

4. Teachers' perceptions of students' identities and learning needs

Four of the eight teachers in our study, across all three schools, referred to ethno-nationalist, xenophobic or racist attitudes among some students. These observations were made in response to our questions about European citizenship.

This tendency was most pronounced among the Coalthorpe teachers and was explained largely in terms of insular and xenophobic tendencies within the relatively homogeneous former mining community where the school is situated, and which had experienced a recent influx of Eastern and Central European migrants, following European Union enlargement in 2004 and 2007.

Students were felt to have exclusive regional and national identities: 'They're British … they're English, they're very much Yorkshire – our kids are so narrow in their own identity, in their own reaction to people' (Ms Clark). She believed it unlikely young people in this community would see themselves as European until 'the next generation'. Racism and xenophobia were linked, according to the teachers, to parental influence and particularly to economic disadvantage. *They* (formerly Black and Asian people, more recently Eastern Europeans) were said by the students to be 'taking jobs away'. Intolerance was believed to be growing as economic conditions worsened. Even when people took holidays in another part of Europe, they were not interested in experiencing another culture, or exposing themselves to a new language:

> Many people haven't been further than Spain, and when they go to Spain they expect to eat British food and everyone to speak English … there's an arrogance within this culture that everyone should be able to speak English and … have fish and chips when they go abroad.
>
> [Ms Clark, Coalthorpe Community College]

Teachers suggested that none of the Coalthorpe students had any sense of European identity, as illustrated in this observation by Ms Shepherd: 'I've never, in all the years I've taught, had a student say "I am a European citizen"'.

Racist and xenophobic beliefs were sometimes coupled with support for the far right British National Party (BNP), who are active in the area, and who fielded a large number of candidates, but won no seats, in the May 2008 local elections. Ms Clark, herself of mixed white British and Pakistani descent, noted how one of her students openly argued for 'repatriation' of non-whites, adding that he would not include her in this policy.

At Lambton School, with a broader social intake and significant numbers of middle class students, teachers sought to explain away Eurosceptic attitudes and xenophobic responses, arguing that students were 'not really racist'; they were 'good kids' but simply lacked the experience of living in a diverse community.

There is no long-standing tradition of BNP activity in the area, although the party fielded a large number of candidates in the 2007 local election, probably with the goal of building support in preparation for the 2009 European elections. Teachers acknowledged that students might also be influenced by xenophobic tendencies in some newspapers, coupled with minimal TV coverage of European affairs, and a significant degree of Euroscepticism among families and in the community.

At the multicultural Hornby Road School, perhaps not surprisingly, teachers did not link xenophobia with lack of exposure to other cultures, yet felt that examining features of the European Union in class was enough to trigger xenophobia: 'Start talking about the Euro and even quite young kids will start to get agitated and xenophobic' (Mr Thompson). Ms James felt that students took the European Union for granted and were not familiar with the benefits that membership brings: 'The kids actually don't think we belong to Europe or that we should belong to Europe'. She suggested that since 'their parents aren't always the best informed about Europe' and the media is often negative, students were likely to be Eurosceptical, and risked adopting more extreme xenophobic positions.

We would argue that lack of factual information leaves students vulnerable to the propaganda of the BNP or, indeed, any political party, and ill-prepared to make a proper assessment of their claims. Within the city, the BNP scored 11.4 per cent of the total vote in the 2007 local elections, winning one seat. Given that a system of proportional representation operates in European elections, the BNP need as little as 10 per cent of the total vote across the region to return an MEP in the 2009 European elections.

Teachers at Hornby Road felt that students had limited knowledge of Europe and the European Union; one suggested it was an important part of the curriculum because:

> You take them out even to another part of [the city] and they'd be lost. Take them to the Dales they'd freak out. ... most kids have only ever been to seaside resorts, you know, even quite well-off kids. They go to Spain and ... think Spain is how it is.
> [Mr Ingram, Hornby Road School]

Concerns about insularity, xenophobia and racism motivated the Coalthorpe teachers to develop a form of citizenship education, which addressed identity; promoted tolerance and respect; and intercultural skills. For them, it was important to explore the possibilities of European identity and citizenship in order to develop skills and attitudes which foster social cohesion. Their students' very insularity threatened to undermine their opportunities to share in the project of a peaceful and prosperous Europe. Global solidarity appeared to trump European identity, even though examining global structures and institutions might also prompt jingoistic responses:

I think we're making some progress [in developing a European dimension] and in making them aware that they're not just English and British but they are members of the Commonwealth – although they all want the empire back when you start talking about that.
[Ms Clark, Coalthorpe Community College]

At both Lambton and Hornby Road Schools it was assumed that students would learn about Europe through history and geography. The study of European institutions and structures, or the means by which decisions are reached in Europe, although part of citizenship education, was far less appealing to students, and therefore something to be avoided or minimized.

On the one hand, teachers saw the value of teaching about European citizenship and belonging; on the other, the EU raises a host of challenges, related to the resistance of young people to Europe and the broader political climate in which teachers and students are working and learning. From the perspectives of their teachers, some young people have identities which need to be expanded through the processes of education. It is these same identities however, which pose real challenges to teachers wishing to find common ground on which to open up dialogue and learning. A tension remains betweenwhat these teachers wish to address and what they do for the sake of expediency.

5. 'Active citizenship', local community and pedagogy

We consider the teachers' emphasis on the local and the implications of this for both curriculum content and pedagogy, discussing the inter-relationship between the two. One reason teachers emphasise the local is because they see local concerns as most relevant to students' lives and interests. Teachers stress the familiarity of local issues as a reason to focus on these; this familiarity allows them to adopt pedagogical approaches where students are collaborating with teachers, to a certain degree, in setting an agenda for learning:

We start with them going out into their community and taking two photographs – one of something they really like about their community and one of something they don't like – and we use that as a lead-in to anti-social behaviour.
[Ms Shepherd, Coalthorpe Community College]

Ms Shepherd was willing to let students take the lead, but she had already decided the focus of the follow-up lessons, namely, examining the consequences of anti-social behaviour. Her colleague, Ms Jessop, also devised an exercise which invited students to think about their concerns, but with an explicitly political agenda of recognising human interdependence, working from inter-personal to international concerns:

> I've been using this diagram for students ... a globe just with concentric circles and in the middle is them ... But then let's think about the local community, and the national community, and the global community ... Always with them at the centre ... how everything relates to them and their lives.
>
> [Ms Jessop, Coalthorpe Community College]

Across all three schools, teachers emphasised student action and engagement in the local community as a first step towards political literacy:

> We are ... trying to get the children to be active, to get them involved, to get them into the community and changing things ... I'm trying to get the kids working at a local level ... I do not want them to think: 'Yeah, well, I got a grade A citizenship, my knowledge is very good but I don't help anybody. I'm just passive'. You've got to be doing it in the classroom and you've got to get them active there and then they'll be active later on.
>
> [Mr Graham, Lambton School]

Active learning in the community was seen to be enjoyable as well as effective, and therefore more motivating to students. As Mr Ingram of Hornby Road School expressed it, 'kids learn from experiences, don't they'.

Teachers at Coalthorpe Community College had less experience of community-based approaches than those at the other two schools. Classroom work had also been largely teacher-centred. Participation in the TEESAEC initiative led this group of teachers to reflect on classroom pedagogies and on the relationship between citizenship knowledge and community engagement:

> Since the project, I think we've learnt that we need to have more active lessons and that we need to have children actually taking action and doing something and using the information that they've learnt. ... It's OK to learn about it, but ... they actually need to do something about it.
>
> [Ms Shepherd, Coalthorpe Community College]

An exclusively academic approach to learning was seen to 'turn the kids off' as one teacher put it; whereas activity-based learning citizenship was seen as inclusive, enabling those with learning difficulties to engage on the basis of equality. A teacher at Coalthorpe, where there was a disproportionately large number of students with learning difficulties, explained that the staff were not in favour of having citizenship as an examination subject, where students would receive grades, since citizenship should not be a subject for which you are graded, but should enable all young people the opportunity to contribute to society. This was a decision about which students had been consulted:

When citizenship was introduced we had a meeting with the student council and they didn't want to do it [the exam]. They felt that citizenship was something that every student should learn, it shouldn't be dependent on whether you are capable of a GCSE [examination at 16 plus] and you shouldn't be graded because everybody should be respected for contributions that they make. You shouldn't be told 'Oh, you're an F grade citizen or you're a D grade citizen'. So they were very, very clear they did not want to do the GCSE and we've respected that.

[Ms Shepherd, Coalthorpe Community College]

Engagement in the local community sometimes involved students learning about local political structures and processes. This was the experience of a group of Lambton students, who campaigned for a youth shelter. They had to present their plans to the local council, lobbying the council to gain financial support. Not only did they learn new skills; the teacher who supported them also wanted them to recognise that they could make a difference:

Working on that youth shelter was really exciting. The kids did it. They did all the work; they did the research; they developed the ICT; they were developing their enquiry skills; they were developing their public speaking skills; they were developing materials to present. All of which required us to talk about: how will we present that material? How can we get our ideas across so that we can justify [our school] getting the £10,000? The youngsters were empowered.

[Mr Graham, Lambton School]

The teacher, who taught a module on human rights, went on to explain that, for him, this was an exercise in children's rights: the students were able to exercise their right to express their opinions and be listened to in a decision which affected them, in line with Article 12 of the UN Convention on the Rights of the Child. He suggested this was a more effective way of learning about human rights than him 'boring them rigid' by lecturing them on the topic. He set out to create a pedagogical process in which the students 'had to think'.

At Hornby Road School, students were encouraged to participate and to improve community life in a different way, not through political processes, but through volunteering: 'We give them opportunities to …become good citizens via the volunteering opportunities we provide them in school' (Ms James).

Here the concept of a 'good citizen' is someone who improves community life by serving others. The students were, nevertheless, learning a similar set of skills to those at Lambton Road, through the activities they were engaged in: planning a Christmas party for seniors and distributing gifts at Easter. They developed skills in planning and organisation; fund-raising; and liaising with different interest groups. Although charitable work might seem a 'safer' option than engagement in local politics, the skills are transferable, and might be equally applied to more overtly political processes. The Hornby Road teachers did not, however, use a rights discourse.

Some teachers stressed political and social awareness; others gave greater emphasis to moral awareness. Those in the former group also stressed that students learn about their rights and their responsibilities and understand how political decisions affect them (especially at the local level). Teachers saw the importance of learning about basic political processes, such as voting, and the work of their local member of parliament.

Learning for citizenship also included studying current news and media debates, particularly if the news item had some local resonance. So, for example, a high profile news story of the abuse and subsequent death of a seventeen-month-old baby, known as Baby P, in the London Borough of Haringey, offered opportunities to consider broader issues, relating to the care and protection of children and the collective responsibilities of citizens:

> The whole function of school for me is how we socialise our young to function in society and ... make that society better ... I think we need an intellectual and social accountability, not just skills-based [teaching]. Teaching citizenship for me it's a very positive move if we teach the sort of citizenship where we address issues like Baby P ... It's not just a blight on Haringey, it's a blight on us in society because there will probably be Baby Ps within half a mile of where we are talking.
>
> [Ms Clark, Coalthorpe Community College]

There was broad alignment between the aims of citizenship education identified by teachers and their preferred pedagogies. Not only did they advocate project work, community-based learning and volunteering, but they also repeatedly stressed that citizenship learning should be accessible to all students, regardless of attainment levels. Active learning was seen to provide opportunities for improving knowledge and understanding, as well as skills. The overall goal was to enable students to be independent learners who can access information via a variety of sources, including the internet.

Group work was seen to be a key means of ensuring maximum participation and cooperation between students, enabling them to take responsibility for their own learning; improve research skills; and manage their own projects. Nevertheless, projects which demand a high degree of responsibility and independence were seen to be more suited to higher attaining students, as were projects which enabled students to make connections between local, national and international concerns and examine these different scales. The approach is designed to foster group cooperation and encourage compassion in students; the emphasis appears to centre on charity, rather than on means by which young people as citizens might work to alleviate poverty by campaigning, for example, for justice in addressing issues such as international debt and international trade:

> The higher ability children do seem to like the global work ... It's an awful lot of research. When we look at poverty ... [groups] research their own charity ... They look at poverty around the world and they do their own [fund-raising] event that they manage themselves, take the money off to the charity, and they love that kind of independence.
> [Ms Shepherd, Coalthorpe Community College]

Teachers also wish to promote discussion, debate and the voicing of student opinions. An essential component of citizenship education, according to the teachers interviewed, is the promotion of critical thinking and freedom of expression in the classroom. Teachers therefore see their role as information providers, particularly on potentially controversial issues. Students are provided with alternative viewpoints and given opportunities to discuss these amongst themselves, usually in small groups, in order to arrive at their own understandings and formulate their own viewpoints: 'It's ... asking them to make an informed judgment on their own – that's the key I think (Mr Patterson, Lambton School). A colleague adds:

> I want to have the children talking, I want them voicing their opinions, I want them justifying their opinions and I want them debating, you know, controversial issues. ... One of the key strands of citizenship is ... enquiry ... that's a skill we want to develop.
> [Mr Graham, Lambton School]

6. Teachers' understandings of citizenship, identity and the nation

Since 2006, before he became Prime Minister, Gordon Brown has been calling for a greater focus on British history in schools, and a range of commentators, including senior government ministers, have focused on the role of schools in creating a united and cohesive society. A number have suggested that the curriculum, notably the teaching of history and citizenship, might be directed to strengthen Britishness and 'British values', promote patriotism, and contribute to the integration of minority communities (Osler, 2009).

As we have shown above, the official citizenship curriculum has quite a strong national focus, although the discourse of the teachers we interviewed focused on the local dimension. The teachers justified their choices with reference to students' needs and identities on the one hand, and the ease with which the local enabled them to adopt their preferred pedagogies judged to be compatible with 'active citizenship'. We invited teachers to discuss whether they judged national identity and the national dimension of citizenship to be significant.

The teachers we spoke with were familiar with the debates about Britishness, and the Prime Minister's perspective. Although the tendency is to focus on the local when teaching citizenship skills and raising contemporary issues, the focus when examining history in secondary schools, appears to be at the level of the nation. One history teacher felt that since the introduction of a national curriculum some 20 years ago, history had been particularly vulnerable to political intervention:

> The national curriculum we follow mostly is British history, but of course that does include Scotland, Wales, Northern Ireland. ... The new A-level course [targeted at students 16-18 years] I'm going to be delivering next year is Britain from 1945 to now ... We've had our syllabus changed over the last 20 years half a dozen times for political advantage. It's all gone British. Even [Prime Minister] Brown feels that's important.
> [Mr Thompson, Hornby Road School]

At Coalthorpe Community College, which until relatively recently has drawn its intake, more or less exclusively, from an apparently homogenous white British working class community, teachers suggested it was important to look at the topic of British identity in the classroom:

> In year 8 we start off talking about our identity – what makes you British, and then we move on to: how does our culture accept people who are not British into our community? ...We look at ... why do we feel British, what makes somebody be British?
> [Ms Shepherd, Coalthorpe Community College]

This teacher went on to explain that, from this starting point, she examines the British justice system and laws; the impact of national politics on the local community; and ways in which students might influence decisions through the process of voting. The importance of voting was also stressed by a teacher at Lambton School, who referred to 'informed voters' who might seek to influence foreign, as well as domestic policy decisions:

> I want them to understand what our country does in the world and the costs we incur doing that. I want them to become informed voters so when [political] parties are saying – we will do this and we will do that – they've got the information to make their own political decision.
> [Mr Patterson, Lambton School]

7. Ambivalence about European but not global citizenship

As we have discussed above, the teachers we interviewed expressed a degree of ambivalence about teaching for European citizenship. Typically, the citizenship curriculum had been designed at school level to begin with the local community in year 7 moving to national and international scales as the students progressed through secondary school:

> [In] year 9 we do global citizenship and they start off looking at the European Union and we start off by looking at the different countries ... We then look at human rights and then we start to look at poverty around the world, and different governments around the world, and democracy against dictatorship. Then in year 10 we revisit some of the stuff we did in year 7 and 8, but at a higher level ... In year 11 we come back to global citizenship, the UN and the Commonwealth.
>
> [Ms Shepherd, Coalthorpe Community College]

The tendency, in all three schools, was to focus, in citizenship classes, on different European countries and cultures. Teachers explained that students find this more interesting than studying the EU and its institutions. Those who stressed the importance of the EU, emphasised examining the philosophy behind its creation without going into too much detail, arguing that students generally find this topic complicated and dry. European identity offered, for some teachers, a potential antidote to the ethno-nationalism espoused by some students.

Participation in the TEESAEC project provoked debate among the teachers about the importance of teaching about the EU, but the teachers remained ambivalent, largely because they found it difficult to make the connection between the EU and students' everyday lives. Given the low profile of EU matters in the British media (even at the time of writing, a matter of weeks before the June 2009 European elections) their ambivalence is understandable. In the face of Eurosceptic sentiments within each of the major political parties and a consequent avoidance of European issues among party political spokespersons, teachers face a difficult task.

Those few teachers who had previous experience of teaching about the EU, through history, confirmed that some students were resistant:

> If I do Britain [19]45 to now ... we'll talk about the European Union because its impact... over the last 36 years has been significant. Kids find it boring. They find it boring. They don't find it interesting, *other than to vent prejudices*. It's quite a good one for starting an argument if you want to raise it.
>
> [Mr Thompson, Hornby Road School, our emphasis]

Teaching about Europe was therefore a challenging task, particularly in terms of finding an effective methodology to encourage students to be open-minded and engaged. In addition, teachers felt that they lacked adequate training and resources. This was cited as a key reason as to why the teachers opted to participate in the TEESAEC project, since they welcomed the WebQuest resources. However, they judged the materials too complicated, overly detailed and lacking differentiation to meet the needs of mixed-ability groups. Teachers therefore found it difficult to keep students on-task and argued that the materials did not encourage critical thinking, since students resorted to cutting and pasting in order to answer difficult questions. Since the materials encouraged individual rather than cooperative learning, teachers found the approach incompatible with their own philosophies of learning and with the official aims of citizenship education.

Teachers did not express the same ambivalence about teaching global issues. The interviews suggest that history teachers were at ease, for example, in addressing the Arab/Israeli conflict and the U.S. civil rights movements. Within geography classes, they mentioned population, development, and environmental issues, including carbon footprints and the Kyoto agreement. Complex economic and political issues in countries such as Rwanda and Zimbabwe were also part of the curriculum. Within designated citizenship classes students studied human rights, poverty, and an examination of different forms of government, comparing and contrasting, for example, democracy and dictatorship. They also examined the institutions of the Commonwealth and the United Nations. All these global issues contain their own complexities, tensions and challenges. It is possible that some teachers lacked sufficient understanding of Britain's position as an EU member-state; shared some of the scepticism in the wider community; or recognised tensions that remain within the European project.

8. Conclusion

It is within the local community that most individuals first engage as citizens. Teachers from all three schools were conscious of this, and, given that they stressed the need for 'active citizenship', it is perhaps not surprising they gave considerable weight to the local dimension of citizenship during the interviews and in the selection of curriculum content. The pedagogical choices they make, which depend heavily on community engagement and learning, reinforce this emphasis on the local.

The current citizenship national curriculum for England, implemented in secondary schools from 2008, places considerable weight on both national identity and national political institutions and processes. While it addresses the EU, it gives it relatively little attention, and does not address European identity. Teachers, particularly those working in predominantly white schools and communities, recognise the importance of exploring a broad-based understanding of British identity and Britishness. Interestingly, this was emphasised more in the working class Coalthorpe Community College, than in Lambton School where there is a greater number of middle class students.

Developing an inclusive concept of Britishness was not such a preoccupation in the multicultural city environment of Hornby Road School, where it was accepted as given. This is in itself interesting, given the preoccupation of political leaders to emphasise the need for minorities to integrate. Teachers saw the problem in different terms, emphasising the need to challenge the insular and sometimes racist attitudes of some white students, as a central aspect of the project of social cohesion.

The teachers we interviewed, who had certainly moved out of their comfort zones to participate in the TEESAEC project and teach about the European Union, recognised the importance of the EU in terms of its impact on the lives of those living in Britain. Their ambivalence seems to stem from three concerns: an unfavourable political climate; student hostility or indifference; and, most importantly, an apparent incompatibility of matching a seemingly remote EU with students' everyday lives and with preferred pedagogies that focus on active, community-based learning and cooperative group work.

This last concern was perhaps the strongest and was compounded by a perceived lack of appropriate teaching materials. This factor may be of particular significance, given that similar reservations were not expressed when addressing the global dimension to citizenship, for which there appear to be adequate attractive resources (Ibrahim, 2005).

The teachers interviewed were anxious to contribute to the debate addressing different scales on which citizenship learning can be conceived: local, national, European, and global. Their first priority was to respond to their students' needs, interests and identities. Participation in the TEESAEC project enabled the teachers to think more about the broader European project, particularly in terms of how it might be used to encourage tolerance and respect, challenge racism and promote social cohesion.

References

Brookes, R.M. & Holford, J.A.K. (2009). Citizenship, learning and education: Themes and issues. *Citizenship Studies,* 13(2), 85–103.

Edwards, J. & Fogelman, K. (Eds.). *Developing citizenship in the curriculum.* London: David Fulton.

Department for Education and Skills (2007). *Curriculum review: Diversity and citizenship (Ajegbo report).* PPSLS/D35/0107/14. London: DfES.

Ibrahim, T. (2005). Global citizenship education: mainstreaming the curriculum. *Cambridge Journal of Education*, 35 (2), 177−194.

Macpherson, W. (1999). *The Stephen Lawrence inquiry*. London: Stationery Office.

Osler, A. (2000). The Crick Report: difference, equality and racial justice. *Curriculum Journal*, 11 (1) 25−37.

Osler, A. (2008). Citizenship education and the Ajegbo report: Re-imagining a cosmopolitan nation. *London Review of Education*, 6(1), 11−25.

Osler, A. (2009). Patriotism, multiculturalism and belonging: Political discourse and the teaching of history. *Educational Review*, 61(1), 85−100.

Osler, A. & Starkey, H. (2006). Education for democratic citizenship: a review of research, policy and practice 1995−2005. *Research Papers in Education* 21(4), 433−466.

Qualifications and Curriculum Authority (QCA) (1998). *Education for citizenship and the teaching of democracy in schools (Crick report)*. London: QCA.

Qualifications and Curriculum Authority (QCA) (2007a). *The National Curriculum. Citizenship: Programme of study for key stage three and attainment target* (p. 27−39). London: QCA. Retrieved 9 May 2009 from http://curriculum.qca.org.uk/uploads/ QCA-07-3329-pCitizenship3_tcm8-396.pdf?return=/key-stages-3-and-4subjects/ citizenship/key-stage3/index.aspx%3Freturn%3D/key-stages-3-and-4/subjects/ citizenship/index.aspx

Qualifications and Curriculum Authority (QCA) (2007b). The National Curriculum. Citizenship: Programme of study for key stage four and attainment target (p. 41−49). Retrieved 9 May 2009 from http://curriculum.qca.org.uk/uploads/QCA-07-3330-pCitizenship4_tcm8-397.pdf?return=/key-stages-3-and-4/subjects/citizenship/ keystage4/index.aspx

Qualifications and Curriculum Authority (QCA) (2007c). *The National Curriculum. History: Programme of study for key stage three and attainment target* (p. 111−119). London: QCA. Retrieved 9 May 2009 from http://curriclum.qca.org.uk/uploads/ QCA-07-3335-p_History3_tcm8-189.pdf?return=/key-stages-3-and-4/subjects/ history/index.aspx

Rollock, N. (2009). *The Stephen Lawrence inquiry 10 years on: An analysis of the literature*. London: Runnymede Trust. Retrieved 11 May 2009 from http://www. runnymedetrust.org/uploads/publications/pdfs/Stephen LawrenceInquiryReport-2009.pdf

Tomlinson, S. (2009). Multicultural education in the United Kingdom. In J.A. Banks (Ed.), *The Routledge International Companion to Multicultural Education*. London: Routledge.

European Union Citizenship Socialization and Education

Henk Dekker & Sanne A.M. Rijkhoff

1. Introduction

What is 'good' European Union citizenship and how is it promoted? What do citizens of the European Union think and feel about the European Union? How knowledgeable are they about the European Union? What is the contribution of secondary school education to this knowledge? These are the key questions for this contribution, in which we also contextualize and reflect on the research results presented in the previous contributions.

2. European Union citizenship

Citizenship is both a legal concept and a political-psychological concept. The legal concept focuses on laws and the legal status, rights and duties of citizens. In the political-psychological concept of citizenship, on which this contribution focuses, the individual and his/her orientations and behaviors are the center of interest. Political-psychological citizenship includes the whole of knowledge and insights, beliefs, opinions, preferences, attitudes, emotions, values, behavioral intentions, and behaviors of an individual in relation to the political system of which he/she is a member. This citizenship has high relevance for both the individual – citizenship may be a fundamental part of the individual's sense of positive identity (Bloom, 1993) – and for the political system, since the development, maintenance, change and survival of a political system depends on the existence of demonstrable support of a considerable part of its constituents (Citrin & Sides, 2004).

Citizenship in the political-psychological sense of the word has different levels, e.g. minimal and advanced. The scale ranges from 'very bad' citizens to 'very good' citizens. What makes an individual a 'good' citizen, is a normative question. Empirical research can reveal the various views on 'good' citizenship among elites and citizens and can also reveal how many citizens meet these ideal-type expectations.

The two main ideal-types of 'good' democratic citizenship parallel the two ends of the democracy scale, ranging from a simple form of representative democracy to a participatory democracy. Participatory democracy requires more and other orientations and behaviors than representative democracy (Dekker, 1996). The set of orientations and behaviors of basic, minimal or 'good enough citizenship' (Dahl,

1992) includes being sufficiently politically informed, sharing the values of democracy, and voting in elections (Theiss-Morse, 1993). Political ignorance, democratic indifference, and political apathy are considered antitheses of democratic citizenship.

'Good' European Union citizenship, as it is described in various documents of the European Union, includes knowledge about the European Union and its establishment, development, goals, functioning, institutions and bodies, decision making, multicultural characteristics, place in Europe and in the world. Furthermore, citizens should have a feeling of belonging to a European community, a sense of European 'identity', and an appreciation of the other Europeans living at the other side of the national frontiers. They are also expected to share the values of pluralism, tolerance, friendship between people, social justice and respect for human rights. Finally, they are expected to be willing to participate and to vote in the elections for the European Parliament (Dekker, 1993ab).

3. European Union citizenship socialization

The European Union has taken two categories of measures to promote this European Union citizenship: offering opportunities for exercising this citizenship, and socialization and education. The assumption is that individuals become European citizens by personal experiences and by accepting informative and affective messages from relevant others.

The opportunities for exercising European citizenship which are offered include direct elections for the European Parliament, a right of petition, access to the European Court of Justice, professional, consumer, or other organizational representation in the Economic and Social Committee, regional representation in the Committee of the Regions, and access to a European Ombudsman.

Socialization and education activities to promote European Union citizenship include offering public information, introducing and applying symbols and rituals, and promoting a European dimension in education and other youth-related activities. Public information is offered by means of a constant flow of brochures, books and magazines, a large number of general and specialized websites, and guided visits to the European Parliament and other institutions. The aims of these activities are to bring the European Union closer to the minds of the citizens, to improve support for the European Union, and to strengthen the willingness to vote in the elections for the European Parliament. Symbols, e.g., the European Union flag and anthem, and rituals, e.g. the Europe Day, aim to facilitate identification with and to create positive emotions with respect to the European Union. The European dimension in education aims to improve knowledge and insight in the European Union and to strengthen positive atttudes towards the European Union and its member states and peoples. It is promoted by, for instance, co-financing the development of curricula about the European Union, summer schools for European groups of participants, and study abroad and exchange programmes for students, teachers and school administrators. If the European project 'is to make progress, it needs ambition and enthusiasm, and commitment on the part of young people to the values on which it is based' (European Commission in the 2001 White Paper on Youth of the European Commission, p. 4). This said, education continues to be the responsibility of the member states.

4. European Union citizenship in practice

Since 1973, the European Commission has been monitoring the evolution of public opinion in the Member States and thereby studying whether or not the institutional and socialization and education measures to promote European citizenship are effective. These (standard, special and flash) Eurobarometers among representative samples of citizens in all member-states show that the measures to promote European citizenship were not very effective (although we should not forget that also many other factors influence the acquisition of orientations and behavior). The following findings illustrate this observation.

Only half of the European Union citizens consider their country's membership a good thing (52%). Only half of the European Union citizens think their country has on balance benefited from membership (55%), while one third think that their country has not benefited from EU membership (32%). Less than half of the Europeans have a positive image of the EU (43%), while almost four out of ten have a neutral image (38%) and almost two out of ten a negative image (17%). Around four out of ten tend not to trust the European Union (40%), the European Parliament (37%), the European Commission (36%), and the European Central Bank (40%). A majority of Europeans believe that the European Union plays a positive role in only 2 of the 15 policy areas included in the survey: protecting the environment (51%) and research (51%). Only small minorities believe that the European Union plays a positive role in the two issues facing their country that are considered most important: the economic situation (36%) and unemployment (24%). (European Commission, 2009a; N = 27.218 randomly selected citizens of the European Union aged 15 years and above).

Five months before the 2009 elections, half of the Europeans were not interested in the elections for the European Parliament (53%). Less than four out of ten citi-

zens had the intention to vote (34%) (European Commission 2009; Standard Eurobarometer 71 European Parliament; N = 27.218). The actual turnout was also very
low (43%), ranging from 91% in Luxembourg to 20% in Slovakia. EU-wide turnout dropped from 62% in 1979 to 43% in 2009 (1984: 59%, 1989: 58%, 1994:
57%, 1999: 50%, 2004: 45%; European Parliament and TNS, 2009).

5. Knowledge about the European Union

Knowledge about the European Union, the variable of focus in the rest of this contribution, is an important ingredient of normative democratic and European citizenship. It is also a necessary condition for comprehending the contents of public debate and for informed participation. Knowledge also tends to affect the content of
opinions, preferences, attitudes, behavioral intentions and behavior. From research
we know that more informed citizens would frequently develop different opinions
and preferences and perform different behavior – opinions, preferences and behavior that would often benefit currently less-informed citizens (Prior, 2002, p. 528;
Gilens, 2001; Kinder, 2004). A lack of knowledge – 'I don't know enough about
the European Parliament'- and a shortage of information – 'I am not sufficiently
informed to go to vote' are the most cited reasons for not willing to go and vote for
the European Parliament (64% and 59% respectively; European Commission
2009b; see also Blais, 2007).

Knowledge about the European Union has been measured in only a few Eurobarometers. In general, Europeans do not possess much knowledge about the European Union. The following findings illustrate this observation.

Only half of the Europeans knew the correct answer to the 'true or false' question
on the exact number of Member States (52%). Seven out of ten indicated correctly
that Switzerland is not a member (68%). Three out of ten knew that the euro zone is
composed of fifteen members (29%). Half of the respondents knew that, every six
months, a different country takes over the Presidency of the Council of the European Union (51%). Relatively many Europeans didn't answer these questions at all
(24%, 18%, 34%, and 28% respectively). Citizens in Luxembourg and Slovenia
(which held the Presidency of the Council at the time of the survey) were the most
knowledgeable; they received the highest score on this 'objective knowledge quiz'
consisting of these four knowledge questions. Respondents in the United Kingdom
scored the lowest (European Commission 2008b; Part 4 The European Union and
its citizens, N = 30.170).

Six out of ten Europeans did not to know what 'citizenship of the European Union' means: one-third have heard the term but were not sure what exactly it means

(37%) and two out of ten have never heard the term (22%). Surprisingly, with a few exceptions, citizens from the new member states said they were more familiar with the term than those from the previous member states. Two-thirds of the respondents from the 27 member states considered themselves not well informed or not at all informed about their rights as citizens of the European Union (68%). A small majority knew the correct answers to the three objective knowledge questions about becoming a European citizen (56%). Less than two out of ten respondents were able to correctly identify as true or false each of the six propositions regarding the fundamental rights that they hold as citizens of the European Union (18%) (European Commission, 2008; Flash Eurobarometer 213, European Union Citizenship, N = 27.000).

The Eurobarometer studies focus on low-level knowledge, i.e. memorization and reproduction. Middle-level knowledge – solving problems that have just one correct solution – and high-level knowledge – solving problems that theoretically have more than one correct solution – have not been studied. The studies also focus on concrete knowledge of specific objects rather than theoretical knowledge of concepts and theories.

Measuring political knowledge is not an easy task. The methodology of political knowledge research tries to find solutions for the many pitfalls (Delli Carpini & Keeter, 1993; Mondak, 2001; Mondak and Anderson, 2004; Luskin and Bullock, 2004).

6. Explanations for variance in knowledge.

An important question is why one individual has much knowledge about the European Union while an other has almost no European Union knowledge. How can we explain these differences in knowledge about the European Union? We have not found any study that answers this question. The Eurobarometer studies are descriptive and do not offer multivariate analyses.

Studies that aimed to explain variance in political knowledge in general – usually knowledge of politics in the respondents' own country – have revealed various important explanatory variables. We see three categories of explanations for variance in political knowledge. The first category is the cognitive ability to receive and process political information. The second category of explanations are motivations to receive and process political information such as interest in politics, being curious and enjoy knowing what is going on in politics and expecting direct personal benefits that arise from political knowledge. The third category of explanations includes opportunities to receive political information. Gender is a background variable. People acquire political knowledge if they are able, motivated, and invited to do it.

The opportunities to receive information about the European Union are limited. Mass media and school offer probably the most opportunities. Out of five informative media, television is most preferred by young Europeans aged 15-24 (65%). Close to half of the young Europeans (48%) and over half of European students (54%) also select the Internet as their preferred information medium for political matters (the survey question asked for two media). Television receives the most trust from the young Europeans (64%). Four out of ten young Europeans (42%) and close to half of European students (48%) also express most trust in the Internet (the survey question asked for 2 media) (European Commission, 2009; Special Eurobarometer 308).

7. Education about the European Union

Schools try to make future European citizens politically more knowledgeable. One way to bring the European Union in the classroom is to offer a series of lessons about the European Union. Crucial for those who design and develop a series of lessons is asking what makes such a series of lessons succesful. Unfortunately we do not know much about the way people learn about the European Union due to the lack of explanatory empirical studies in this field. There is somewhat more knowledge about important determinants of political learning in general. Key variables are interest or curiosity and perceiving personal benefits from knowing more. How succesful teaching about the European Union is in practice, has hardly been studied and we have not found a recently published empirical study in this field.

The studies presented in this volume are rare exceptions. The studies report about a new teaching and learning project for secondary-school students (and teachers) and the research of its effectiveness. Computer-assisted guided self-discovery and problem solving are key characteristics of the WebQuest lesson series. Students work autonomously in pairs with the WebQuest provided on a computer. They work exclusively with online material which is issue oriented. There are many reasons for computer-assisted education. One is that many young people prefer the Internet as their information medium for political matters and have most trust in the Internet (European Commission, 2009b). Research has shown that learning with Internet-based WebQuest can be effective (Manzel, 2007). One of the foundations for self-learning is Self-Determination Theory. This theory states that ' ... intrinsic motivation and integrated extrinsic motivation are most likely to be evident when individuals experience supports for competence, autonomy and relatedness' (Ryan

& Deci, 2000, p. 74). The problem-solving orientation was selected because of the ambition to improve not only factual knowledge but also conceptual knowledge and to reach the level of insight and understanding (Weisseno, 2004). At the core of the lessons is a concrete issue rather than the institutions; the designers of the series of lessons expected that students think that lessons about institutions must be 'boring'. The issue of the case study was reduction of CO_2 exhaust emissions. This issue was selected because it was expected that students consider this issue very important for their own and relevant others' life.

The research among more than 1000 secondary school students was carried out in five countries (Germany, the Netherlands, Switzerland, Austria and Estonia) and included a pre- and post-test and experimental and control groups. Conceptual knowledge about the European Union was the dependent variable and was measured by 53 multiple-choice items with four answer options each (in Germany and Switzerland the scale was reduced). All items were coded dichotomous (correct and incorrect). The independent variables in the post-test included knowledge at the pre-test, method of teaching (WebQuest or other), school type, gender, attachment to the EU, attitude towards the EU, interest in the EU, emotion with respect to the EU, parental cultural capital or socialization, migration background, and membership of youth and political associations.

The findings show that generally the WebQuest lessons were not effective or not more effective than the other types of lessons in the control group. The post-test knowledge scores were even lower than the pre-test ones (in the Netherlands and Switzerland). The most important predictor of the post-test knowledge was the pre-test knowledge (in Germany, the Netherlands and Switzerland). The 'good' news is that the percentage of students who were satisfied with their level of knowledge about the European Union increased considerably, whereas the number of students who still wanted to know more about the European Union stayed almost the same, and that less students thought that they know nothing or little about the European Union (in the Netherlands). The school teachers involved in the project in the United Kingdom welcomed the WebQuest resources but judged them not very positive, while most teachers in the Netherlands involved in the project were quite enthusiastic about the WebQuest lessons and reported active students' involvement.

8. Conclusion

Eurobarometer studies among representative samples of citizens in all member-states show that European Union citizenship has not been well developed. In general, Europeans do not possess much factual knowledge about the European Union.

The studies presented in this volume report about an innovative teaching project for secondary-school students. Computer-assisted guided self-discovery and problem solving are key characteristics of the WebQuest lesson series. Research among more than 1000 secondary school students in five countries showed that these lessons were not effective or not more effective than other types of lessons.

The European Union's future depends on the support and participation of its citizens. For those who are in favour of the European Union there is still a lot of work to be done to improve citizenship of the European Union. For those who are in favour of a well-informed European Union citizenry also much work is left to be done. The methodology of European Union knowledge research and the methodology of teaching about the European Union still have to answer important questions. What is the best way to measure concrete and theoretical knowledge about the European Union and to explain variance in this knowledge? What are the main determinants of European Union knowledge and which explanatory theory has most empirical evidence? What is the most effective way to teach young Europeans about the European Union? The former member of the European Parliament Larive (1990) once wrote: 'Proper education is the heartbeat of European integration'.

References

Blais, A. (2007). Turnout in Elections. In R. Dalton & H.-D. Klingemann (eds.), *The Oxford Handbook of Political Behavior* (p. 621−635). Oxford, UK: Oxford University Press.

Bloom, W. (1993). *Personal Identity, National Identity, and International Relations.* Cambridge, UK: Cambridge University Press.

Citrin, J. & Sides, J. (2004). Can Europe Exist Without Europeans? Problems of Identity in a Multinational Community. In M.G. Hermann (ed.), *Advances in Political Psychology.* Volume 1 (p. 41−70). Oxford, UK: Elsevier.

Dahl, R.A. (1992). The Problem of Civic Competence. *Journal of Democracy* 3(4), 45−59.

Dekker, H. (1993). European citizenship: a political-psychological analysis. In M. Montané & I. Bordas (eds.), *The European Dimension in Secondary Education* (p. 41−56). Barcelona: Col.legi de Doctors i Llicenciats en Filosofia i Lletres i en Ciencies de Catalunya.

Dekker, H. 1996. Democratic citizen competence: political-psychological and political socialization research perspectives. In R. F. Farnen, H. Dekker, R. Meyenberg & D. B. German (eds.), *Democracy, Socialization, and Conflicting Loyalties in East and West* (p. 386−410). New York, N.Y.: St. Martin's Press.

Delli Carpini, M. & Keeter, S. (1993). Measuring political knowledge: putting first things first. *American Journal of Political Science* 37(4), 1179-1206.

European Commission (2001). *White Paper A New Impetus for European Youth.* COM(2001)681final. Brussels: Commission of the European Communities.

European Commission (2008a). *Flash Eurobarometer 213, European Union Citizenship, Analytical Report.* Brussels: European Commission.

European Commission (2008b). *Standard Eurobarometer 69; Part 4 The European Union and its citizens.* Brussels: European Commission.

European Commission (2009a). *Standard Eurobarometer 71, European Parliament.* Brussels: European Commission.

European Commission (2009b). *Special Eurobarometer 308, The Europeans in 2009.* Brussels: European Commission.

European Parliament and TNS. http://www.europarl.europa.eu/parliament/archive /elections2009/en/turnout_en.html.

Gilens, M. (2001). Political Ignorance and Collective Policy Preferences. *American Political Science Review* 95, 379-396.

Kinder, D. (2004). Pale Democracy: Opinion and Action in Postwar America. In E. D. Mansfield & R. Sisson (eds.), *The Evolution of Political Knowledge: Theory and Inquiry in American Politics* (p. 60–88). Columbus, OH: Ohio State University Press.

Larive, J. (1990). Proper education is the heartbeat of European integration. *ESHA Magazine* 2, 28-31.

Luskin, R.C. & Bullock, J. (2004). Re (:)Measuring Political Sophistication. Paper. http://www.allacademic.com//meta/p_mla_apa_research_citation/0/8/2/5/7/pages82573/ p82573-1.php

Manzel S. (2007a). *Kompetenzzuwachs im Politikunterricht: Ergebnisse einer Interventionsstudie zum Kernkonzept Europa.* Muenster: Waxmann.

Manzel, S. (2007b). Politikunterricht zum Mehrebenensystem Europa mit einem instruktional-konstruktivistischen WebQuest – Ergebnisse einer Studie. In P. Massing (Hrsg.), *Wirkungsforschung zur politischen Bildung im europäischen Vergleich* (p. 7–25). Schwalbach/Ts: Wochenschau Verlag.

Mondak, J. J. (2001). Developing valid knowledge scales. *American Journal of Political Science,* 45 (1), 224-238.

Mondak, J. J. & Anderson, M. R. (2004). The knowledge gap: A reexamination of gender-based differences in political knowledge. *The Journal of Politics* 66, 492-512.

Prior, M. (2002). Political Knowledge after September 11. *Political Science & Politics* 35(3), 523–529.

Ryan, R.M. & Deci, E.L. (2000). Self-Determination Theory and the Facilitation of Intrinsic Motivation, Social Development, and Well-Being. *American Psychologist* 55(1), 68–78.

Theiss-Morse, E. (1993). Conceptualizations of good citizenship and political participation. *Political Behavior* 15(4), 355–369.

Weisseno, G. (2004). Konturen einer europazentrierten Politikdidaktik; Europäische Zusammenhänge verstehen lernen. In G. Weisseno (Hrsg.), *Europa verstehen lernen; Eine Aufgabe des Politikunterrichts* (p. 108–125). Bonn: Bundeszentrale für politische Bildung.

Authors

Professor Dr Henk Dekker is Professor of Political Socialization and Integration in the Faculty of Social and Behavioural Sciences, Institute of Political Science, Leiden University, Netherlands.
E-mail: dekkerh@fsw.leidenuniv.nl

Valentin Eck, MA, is a researcher in the Department of Political Science, University of Education, Karlsruhe, Germany.
E-mail: eck@ph-karlsruhe.de

Professor Dr Reinhold Gaertner is Professor in the Department of Political Science at the University of Innsbruck, Austria. He researches right wing popularism and extremism, Austria's political system, and comparative politics.
E-mail: Reinhold.Gaertner@uibk.ac.uk

Dr Bernhard Natter is a faculty member in the Department of Political Science at the University of Innsbruck, Austria. His fields of research are political theory and civic education.
E-mail: bernhard.natter@uibk.ac.at

Professor Dr Audrey Osler is Founding Director of the Centre for Citizenship and Human Rights Education at the University of Leeds, UK. Her research addresses citizenship, social justice and education policy.
E-mail: A.H.Osler@leeds.ac.uk

Professor Dr Volker Reinhardt is head of the political and democratic education team at the Institute for Pedagogy, Professionalism and School Culture in the University of Teacher Education Central Switzerland, Lucerne.
E-mail: volker.reinhardt@phz.ch

Sanne A.M. Rijkhoff, MA, is research assistant in the Faculty of Social and Behavioural Sciences, Institute of Political Science, at Leiden University, Netherlands.
E-mail: rijkhoffsam@fsw.leidenuniv.nl

Dr Nicola Savvides is research officer in the Centre for Citizenship and Human Rights Education, University of Leeds, UK.
E-mail: n.savvides@education.leeds.ac.uk

Marti Taru, MA, is researcher at the Institute of International and Social Studies, Tallinn University, Estonia and doctoral student in the Department for Political Science, Helsinki University, Finland.
E-mail: marti.taru@gmail.com

Monika Waldis is research collaborator, University of Teacher Education of the University of Applied Sciences Northwestern Switzerland and Centre for Democracy Aarau (ZDA) in Aarau, Switzerland.
E-mail: monika.waldis@fhnw.ch

Professor Dr Georg Weisseno is Professor in the Department of Political Science, University of Education, Karlsruhe, Germany. His research addresses civic education.
E-mail: weisseno@ph-karlsruhe.de

Professor Dr Béatrice Ziegler is head of the Centre for Political Education and History Didactics, University of Teacher Education of the University of Applied Sciences Northwestern Switzerland and the Centre for Democracy Aarau (ZDA) in Aarau.
E-mail: beatrice.ziegler@fhnw.ch

Sabine Manzel

Kompetenzzuwachs im Politikunterricht

Ergebnisse einer Interventionsstudie
zum Kernkonzept Europa

Politikdidaktische Forschung, Band 1
2007, 284 Seiten, br., 24,90 €,
ISBN 978-3-8309-1784-7

Die Interventionsstudie entstand im Rahmen der bildungspolitischen
Debatten um den domänenspezifischen Kompetenzerwerb an Schulen
und in Anlehnung an Leistungsmessungen wie PISA und die IEA-Studie
zur politischen Bildung. Grundlagen bilden der kognitive Kompetenz-
begriff von Eckhard Klieme, der instruktional-konstruktivistische Lehr-
Lernansatz für internet-based instruction aus der Pädagogischen Psychologie, politikwissenschaftliche Fachkonzepte und politikdidaktische
Prinzipien für politische Urteilsbildung. Die Ergebnisse der quasi-
experimentellen Studie zum Kernkonzept Europa zeigen signifikant,
dass die internetbasierte Lehr-Lernumgebung WebQuest zu höheren
kognitiven Outcomes beim politischen Urteilen führt als alltäglicher
Politikunterricht.

Waxmann

MÜNSTER · NEW YORK · MÜNCHEN · BERLIN

Waxmann

Anne Sliwka, Martina Diedrich,
Manfred Hofer (Hrsg.)

Citizenship Education

Theory – Research – Practice

2006, 224 pages, pb, € 24,90,
ISBN 978-3-8309-1608-6

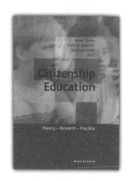

More and more people feel that they cannot leave their lives to be governed by democratic institutions alone. They want to take charge themselves, be involved and have a say in their community – in short, live their lives as active citizens. Citizenship, however, is not a given. Like most things, it needs to be learned, and citizenship education aims to facilitate just that.

For students, citizenship education means more than merely learning *about* citizenship and democracy. Citizenship education means learning *through* practicing citizenship inside and outside the school. One model for that is service learning, first conceived in North America but now also taking root in other parts of the world. Service learning combines service and learning by linking community service and reflection about it in class.

The present volume grounds citizenship education theoretically, presents empirical research about its long-term effects and gives examples of how it works in practice.

Contributions by John Annette, Monika Buhl, Martina Diedrich, Schima Hassan-Beik, Andrew Furco, Gerhard Himmelmann, Manfred Hofer, Klaus Koopmann, Hans Peter Kuhn, Elena Marta, Bruce Maxwell, Cynthia Miller-Idriss, Peter Noack, Hans Oswald, John Potter, Maura Pozzi, Roland Reichenbach, Christina Saß, Anne Sliwka, Heinz Reinders, James Youniss.

MÜNSTER · NEW YORK · MÜNCHEN · BERLIN

WAXMANN
VERLAG GMBH
Münster · New York · München · Berlin
www.waxmann.com · info@waxmann.com